THE GIRL IN WHITE ARMOR

The Girl in White Armor

THE STORY OF JOAN OF ARC

BY ALBERT BIGELOW PAINE

ILLUSTRATED BY JOE ISOM

THE MACMILLAN COMPANY
NEW YORK
COLLIER-MACMILLAN LIMITED
LONDON

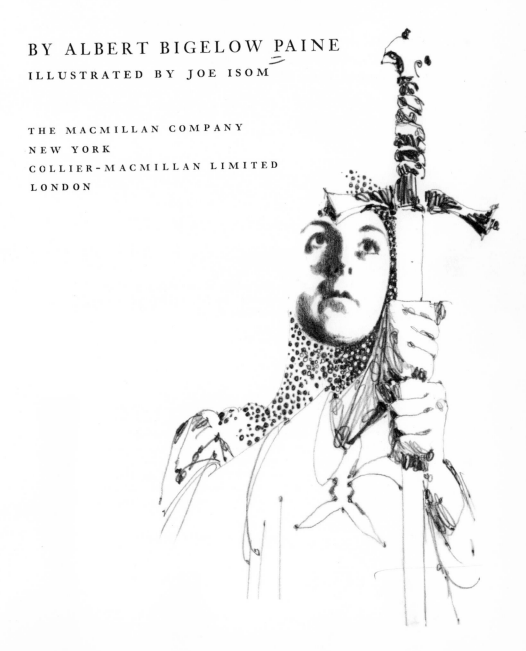

Joan's story as here set down is history. Every episode and detail of it is from the sworn testimony taken at her two trials, and from authentic contemporary chronicles. Nothing is invented. From the first page to the last it is all true.

ALBERT BIGELOW PAINE

1927

CONTENTS

ILLUSTRATIONS

MAPS

PRINCIPAL

CHARACTERS

French

JOAN OF ARC

JACQUES D'ARC, her father

JEAN and PIERRE D'ARC (later, DU LYS), Joan's brothers, who became
her companions-in-arms

DURAND LAXART, Joan's cousin (called "Uncle"), who conducted
her to De Baudricourt

ISABELLE ROMÉE, Joan's mother

JOHN, DUKE OF ALENÇON, military commander of Joan's expedition
to Jargeau

MARIE OF ANJOU, wife of Charles VII of France

JEAN D'AULON, chief of Joan's personal staff

ROBERT DE BAUDRICOURT, governor of Vaucouleurs, from whom
Joan sought help on her mission to the Dauphin

CHARLES VII, Dauphin, later King of France

REGNAULT DE CHARTRES, Archbishop of Reims, Chancellor of France, who influenced the King against Joan

LOUIS DE CONTES, Joan's personal page

JEAN DUNOIS, military commander of Orléans

GUILLAUME DE FLAVY, governor of Compiègne, where Joan was captured

LA HIRE, captain in Joan's army

GEORGES DE LA TRÉMOUILLE, Chief Counselor, who advised Charles VII to forsake Joan

JEAN DE METZ, Joan's companion-in-arms

CHARLES, DUKE OF ORLÉANS, held prisoner in England

FATHER JEAN PASQUEREL, almoner and confessor to Joan

BERTRAND DE POULENGY, Joan's companion-in-arms

ARTHUR OF RICHEMONT, Constable of France, enemy of La Trémouille

English & English Sympathizers

JOHN, DUKE OF BEDFORD, "Regent of France" for King Henry VI of England, who engineered Joan's trial and execution

PHILIP, DUKE OF BURGUNDY, chief French ally of the English

PIERRE CAUCHON, Bishop of Beauvais, Joan's chief judge and tormenter

JEAN D'ESTIVET, prosecutor at Joan's trial

SIR JOHN FASTOLF, English captain at Orléans and Patay

BROTHER MARTIN LADVENU of Rouen, who comforted Joan and gave her last communion

JEAN DE LAFONTAINE, examiner of Joan at her trial

NICOLAS LOISELEUR, canon of Rouen, spy and witness against Joan

JOHN, DUKE OF LUXEMBURG, who sold Joan to the English

G. MANCHON, notary, who kept the only impartial record of Joan's trial

JEAN MASSIEU, bailiff of Joan's prison

WILLIAM DE LA POLE, COUNT OF SUFFOLK, commander of the English at Jargeau, captured by Joan

JOHN, LORD TALBOT, commander of the English at Orléans

RICHARD DE BEAUCAMP, EARL OF WARWICK, Joan's chief jailer at Rouen

I

THE TREE

It grew in Fairyland

A mile and a half to the south of Domrémy, crowning a hill that overlooked the valley of the Meuse, the Tree could be seen from many directions. A mighty beech of great age, it was variously called "Ladies' Lodge" and "Fairy Tree" because according to tradition the ladies of Fairyland sometimes danced there; further, it was said that in the ancient days Pierre Granier of the great castle of Bourlemont whose six towers still rose against the south had walked under the Tree with a radiant lady known only as "Fairy," and never seen elsewhere.

The children found it no trouble to believe these things nor, for that matter, did their parents, for it was a day when myth and legend passed as history. Children had always played under the Ladies' Lodge, and on special days in springtime brought "little loaves baked expressly by their mothers" to eat in the quiet shade. Not far below the Tree a clear spring flowed from the hillside. Its waters were said to be healing; at any rate they were cold and sweet and when the children had drunk their fill they gathered the flowers that grew round about and twined them into wreaths and garlands, to lay before the picture of the Virgin in the village church or to hang on the branches of the Tree for the fairies. Joining hands, they circled under the suspended offerings, singing and dancing, according to a custom of which no one knew the beginning.

They christened her Jeanne, or Jeannette

More than five hundred and fifty years ago one of the children who twined garlands and danced and sang under the Fairy Tree was a little girl who only a few years later would change the fortunes of France. She was the youngest child of Jacques d'Arc and Isabelle Romée (women did not always take the husband's surname), and in the small stone church across the garden they christened her Jeanne, or Jeannette (later, in English, she would be called "Joan," "Joan of Arc").[1]

In Domrémy the birthday of a little peasant girl was held of small account; in after years Joan herself did not know how old she was. Nevertheless, neighbors remembered that she was born on the eve of Epiphany, or Twelfth Night, which is January 6, and the year has been fixed as 1412.

Beyond certain marvels said to have occurred on the night of her birth, of Joan's infancy there is not even a tradition. But of her childhood and the amazing years that followed details are not lacking. Joan herself supplied some of them and playmates, neighbors, companions-in-arms and learned doctors—wit-

---

1. The ancestors of Jacques d'Arc are thought to have come from the village of Arc-en-Barrois fifty miles to the southwest of Domrémy; hence, "d'Arc" (of Arc). Joan's father himself came from Ceffonds, her mother from Vouthon.

nesses sworn to tell the truth—completed the story. The picture is fresh and clear. Nothing else in history compares with it.

A child in a garden

A sturdy little girl, we see her presently following her father to the field or her brothers when they drove the flocks to the pasture—at evening learning her prayers from the devout Isabelle Romée.

"My mother taught me the Pater Noster, Ave Maria and the Credo; no other than she instructed me in my belief" (probably as soon as the child could lisp the words).

The religion of that day was as primitive as it was profound. Everybody believed in demons and witchcraft, evils to be opposed with prayer. Legendary tales of the saints were accepted as gospel; marvelous happenings, told and repeated around the fireside, mingled with Isabelle Romée's moral teaching.

It was a very modest fireside. The low room probably had a clay floor, dry and flinty hard from use. One or two square shuttered holes in the walls served as windows. Some benches were drawn up to the big fireplace and there were beds, or pallets, in the corners. Above was an attic with other beds. All the peasant houses were like that—not squalid, but only humble —that of Jacques d'Arc no different from the others. There may have been more than one room, and a rude connecting stable for the cattle and sheep. All the peasants kept flocks: they were a chief source of income, they grazed on a common pasture and were tended by the children. Because of his sturdy good sense or some gift of leadership Joan's father held office in the community, but his home, his few acres of land, and his flocks were such as were common to all.

"Simple laborers, honest in their poverty, for they were of small means," are the words of a neighbor.

The little girl's home was surrounded by a garden—a sweet place of flowers, vegetables and fruit-bearing trees, divided by a small stream, "The Brook of the Three Sources," that flowing through it crossed the road and went singing into the Meuse. Joan loved the garden and the brook, the sun-dappled flower beds and the light that beamed on the church windows.

When the crosses were carried
along the fields

A little peasant girl like the others, Joan followed the flocks or played with her small companions in the meadows and under the Fairy Tree. Of her early friends there were two that she loved most: Hauviette and Mengette, near neighbors. Little Hauviette may have been the favorite, for she has been called "la préférée." Long afterward she said: "As children Jeannette and I were happy together in her father's house. It was a pleasure for us to sleep in the same bed. Jeannette was good, simple and sweet."

Mengette also told of happy days with Joan and how sometimes they had spun and performed other household duties in company. Joan loved to go to church, she said, and gave alms of whatever she received from her father. Then, of the Tree: "It was a very ancient Tree. From the memory of man one has always seen it there where it is. Each year in the spring, particularly on the Sunday of the Fountains, this Tree was a gathering place. Girls and boys, we came in a troop, bringing small loaves of bread. Often I was with Jeannette. We ate under the Tree, then we went to drink from the Currant Spring. How many times we have laid the cloth under the Tree and eaten together! Afterward we played and danced. Those things still go on; our children do today what we did then."

Another friend of that day told how the little girl's heart had gone out to the poor, how she had slept by the hearth that they might have her bed. And she told of Joan's going to pray in the little chapel of Notre Dame de Bermont on a hill in the woods beyond the adjoining village of Greux.

All remembered the Tree, and one of those who had played there with Joan told of its great beauty and how on Ascension Eve, when the crosses were carried along the fields, the priest went there to chant the service.

Joan herself once referred to the Tree as *le Fau* (a native word for beech) "whence comes the fair May," meaning the branches which the peasants set before their houses on May Day. She had gone there with the other children and twined wreaths for the picture of the Virgin at Domrémy. It was held by old people that fairies came there and that Maire Aubery's wife had seen them. To her knowledge, Joan had never seen fairies near the Tree. Whether she had seen them elsewhere, or not, she did not know. With the others she had hung garlands on the branches. Sometimes she had carried them away afterward, sometimes had left them there. As a child she had danced with other children, though "she had sung more than she had danced."

Of the generations of children that played there probably no one ever loved the spot more than Joan. The wide and fair expanse it commanded appealed not only to her sense of beauty but to something deeper in her, something romantic and glorious, too mystical to be understood. Southward, on the hill above Neufchâteau, rose the six towers of the lords of Bourlemont, seigneurs of Domrémy and Greux, who sometimes with their ladies came to lead the children to the Tree. To the eastward lay the level valley of the Meuse, its placid, irresolute river breaking into channels to form islands, on one of which was another castle, though abandoned, of the lords of Bourlemont. The Meuse has its source in the south and mists rise from its mildly tempered waters. In winter its valley is a weird region of fogs, in spring low-hanging clouds drift above its brilliant green, in June it is a dream valley, its fields under the quiet spell which precedes harvest. In whatever season, to Joan it was a

valley of illusion, of knights on holy errands, of phantom marching armies.

Looking down from the Tree one saw the spire of Coussey, and in another direction Domrémy and Greux—the two villages were really one—with Maxey across the river in Lorraine. Hill and wood shut away the distance but one knew that the loitering river found its way past other villages and came at last to the seat of government, Vaucouleurs (valley of colors), a strong town for all its tranquil name, commanded by Robert de Baudricourt, a sturdy captain hardened in the trade of arms.

Behind Domrémy lay the Bois Chenu, a deep forest that skirted the hillside and stretched back to mysterious depths haunted by wolves and reputed dragons. It was hardly a place for little folks but below it in early summer the slope was red with wild strawberries which the children gathered to eat with their small loaves: and when they had eaten and sung and danced they sat under the shade of the great beech and, looking over the drowsy valley, talked of wonderful things.

Whatever their parents might think of fairies the children had no doubts on the subject. They not only believed in them but were favorable to them. That the fairies had been banished for their sins and forbidden the Tree was not proof that they did not visibly assemble there. Jeanne, wife of Maire Aubery, had seen them! It was said that they sometimes took one up in the air! This happened on Thursday, clearly a magic day. The wreaths suspended on the Tree by the children were sometimes carried away during the night. Who but fairies would take them?

The children discussed these matters and the virtue of charms and amulets. And there was a mandragora, a very potent magic that brought riches and grew somewhere in the ground near the Tree under a hazel bush. But this was evil, a perilous thing to have and not to be spoken of openly. That Joan heard this talk we know from her own story. As a child she probably believed in it for she was as the others.

Yet she was different. Even in that early time when she played and danced and sang with her companions she was often not really with them, but in a land where her playmates did not and could not enter.

She loved the sound of the bells and sometimes when the sexton did not ring them promptly or as much as she thought proper, she reproached him for it, offering to give him wool from her sheep and some of the big round cakes called "moons" if he would do better. Hearing the bells, Joan crossed herself and knelt. When not at her duties she was likely to be in the church at prayer. Her companions rallied her for being so devout. She blushed and did not know how to answer. To escape them she went to the little chapel of Bermont, the remote shrine in the woods beyond Greux. She loved the stillness of the place, having for company the birds that are said to have eaten from her hands.

So we complete the picture of the little peasant girl: diligent, tenderhearted, devout; requiring duty of the bell ringer, offering reward if he performed it; mingling with her companions yet finding alone companionship they could not understand. Said one of these: "Often while we were at play, Jeannette drew apart and spoke to God. The others and myself teased her about it."

Certainly she was different. Her priest of that time declared that there was not her like in the village.

II

THE VOICES

Children dream long dreams

   Thus far the picture has seemed peaceful enough, but a very different one lay just behind it. Almost the first word these children had heard spoken was "war." They had known through their childhood that not far away beyond the hills to the west France was torn by fierce struggles; that bloodshed and famine were there; that their hereditary king was not really a king, never having been crowned, but was little more than a penniless fugitive secluded in some still unconquered corner of his kingdom below the river Loire.

Crushed by a hundred years' warfare with England, France was not even a nation but a medley of warring factions, each, under whatever flag or pretense, striving only for personal gain. Great captains had become bandits; soldiers had become mere marauders; even the peasants had deserted their fields and formed themselves into cruel bands that laid waste far and wide.

Domrémy, on the main road from the south, had plenty of news of these things, brought by traveling merchants, peddlers, begging friars, straggling soldiers. Eager-eyed and open-mouthed, the children gathered round to hear their tales. Then there were the fugitives—hungry and bedraggled refugees—it was for such that Joan sacrificed her bed. Dwellers in the quieter lands along the Meuse knew that the world was stricken; they prepared for the worst.

Governed by that grim soldier, Robert de Baudricourt, at Vaucouleurs, their little province had for the most part escaped hostilities. Cattle had been driven off, but this was mere thievery and once at least the cattle had been recovered. Joan's father and his neighbors leased the abandoned castle—on an island facing the village and connecting with it—as protection for their flocks. Joan herself told of having helped drive the herds to this stronghold. At any alarm the village bells were rung and the cattle were driven there more than once. The old castle also made a fine playground, especially for the game of war.

The children were familiar with the politics of their country. They knew that as a boy their young King, Charles VII, had been driven from Paris and was jestingly called the "King of Bourges" because he had taken refuge in that city. They knew that the King's uncle, the Duke of Orléans, had been basely murdered by John, Duke of Burgundy, and that the present Duke of Orléans, captured at the great French defeat of Agincourt, was still held a prisoner in England. They knew that in his turn John of Burgundy had been assassinated and that his son Philip, with vast domain and wealth and armies, had allied himself with England. They knew that their King's unworthy mother, Isabeau of Bavaria, had disowned her son,[1] married her daughter to King Henry of England and joined in a treaty that would make the son of this marriage ruler of both England and France. They knew that the party of their King was called

---

1. She claimed Charles was illegitimate, and not the son of Charles VI. [ed.]

"Armagnac" after the Gascon noble who had led it and that everywhere Armagnac and Burgundian, at each other's throats, were desolating France.

Stout partisans of their fugitive King, the children were fiercely Armagnac, while Maxey across the river was Burgundian. The boys of Domrémy would occasionally invade Maxey and Joan saw them return with bruised and scratched faces. Thus in a way she was already a part of the struggle for the "Dauphin," as Charles VII was then known to her. To a sensitive imagination like hers the Dauphin was a romantic figure—the wandering prince of legendary tale.

"I had a great and warm zeal that the King should recover his kingdom," are her own words. Children dream long dreams; even before her summons she may have pictured herself offering humble service. We cannot know what she thought but only that her child heart was heavy with the sorrows of her people and the ill fortune of her King.

When Joan was well into her thirteenth year news came of the Battle of Verneuil (August 17, 1424), another defeat for the French army, leaving Charles VII almost without hope. His soldiers, such as were still loyal, were more than ever broken in spirit. The saying was common that two hundred of the English could put to flight a thousand of the French.

"The pity that was of the Kingdom of France"

It was within the year following Verneuil, probably within the month, that Joan received the first word of the work she was to do. On a summer day at the hour of noon, in her father's garden, she saw toward the church a great light and heard a Voice. At that hour she would hardly be spinning or sewing. It would be when dinner had been prepared and she

was waiting a little in the shade for her father and brothers to come from the fields. The Voice came from the direction of the light, "a worthy Voice," full of dignity.

The little girl was greatly frightened and very likely did not remember later just what it was she had seen and heard. But either then or soon after, for the light and the Voice came often, she was told to be a good child, that God would help her and that she would go to the rescue of the King. And the angel spoke to her of "the pity [the sorrow] that was of the kingdom of France."

Telling of this long after, Joan said that on hearing the Voice the third time she knew it to be that of a celestial being—Saint Michael, as she learned—though at first she had great doubts. She also saw a figure, one of stateliness and beauty, accompanied by angels.

At the time she told no one, not even her priest or her pious mother, of these marvelous things. She may have felt that they were for herself alone. She may have feared censure and ridicule. Many strange happenings remain locked in the heart of a sensitive child.

All that we know of Joan's visions is from herself. Whatever their nature—and they have been much discussed—to Joan they were realities that brought her comfort and revealed to her the future. Two or three times a week the light came to her and the Voice she had accepted as that of Saint Michael told her she must go to France.

The little girl may have had dreams of being useful to the King, but now she was filled with fear. The Voice promised her soldiers and told her that Saint Catherine and Saint Margaret would come to her to comfort and counsel her in all that she had to do. They would be good spirits and she must believe what they would say to her: this was "by commandment of the Lord." At such times Joan prostrated herself before the Saint and his angels and after their departure kissed the earth where they had stood, making reverence. It was only a little while later that Joan's other "Voices," Saints Catherine and Margaret, came to her. She once spoke of their appearance at the spring below the Fairy Tree, so it may have been in that quiet place that they first revealed themselves or near the chapel of Bermont. "If I was in a wood I was certain to hear the Voices come."

She did not separate them at first but later knew them very well and could easily tell one from the other; also, they told her their names and seemed to salute her. They were richly crowned and of sweet and gentle speech. They assured her that the King would come into his own and promised to conduct her at last to paradise. She saw their faces, their hair; they exhaled sweet incense. They were so real that at one time or another they confessed her. She embraced their knees at parting, weeping that they would not take her with them.

In time her visitants became less distinct and she was not sure of their individual faces; but their voices remained clear, their message always the same. She had been chosen to restore France, to crown the King and give him back his kingdom. To the Saints Joan pledged her maidenhood "for so long that it pleased God"; that is, until her mission should be ended.

Joan was no pale visionary of delicate health and nerves. She was a hardy country girl of great endurance, capable and with plenty of temper and determination, as we shall see later on; but being also deeply devout she was moved to accept whatever came as by divine command.

Keeping the great secret

During four years and more the visions and Voices continued to come before Joan was ready for her work. How did a girl in the interval from thirteen to seventeen manage to keep that great secret shut up in her heart?

Our story of those years is rather meager. We know that she was less often at play with her companions after knowing that she must "go to France." When she was with them it was in a quieter fashion.

"Come and dance with us, Joan, one would think you were a saint!"

But though she gladly sang with them she joined less and less in their gay dancing. One of those who knew her testified: "She was not a dancer; many times while the others danced and sang she went to pray." This would be after she had begun to hear the Voices; she had slipped away to commune with them. "Consoled the sick, gave alms to the poor," are the words of another. "I experienced her goodness, for as a child I was ill and Jeannette attended me."

Yet she seemed to remain much as she had always been except that as the years passed and she grew taller, stronger, handsomer, she became also more earnest, more grave.

To this day life in Domrémy is primitive; girls still spin with the distaff as they follow their flocks to the field. Yet it was far more simple in Joan's time. In that day there was no such thing as a book or paper to pick up at a leisure moment. Printing was still unknown; hardly anybody could read or needed to. The humble life of the village was varied only by the arrival of a mendicant priest, a peddler or straggling wanderers bringing word of some new raid by the Burgundians and always of the declining fortunes of the King. For leisure one could gossip with a neighbor, walk by the river or go to the church for prayer. During these years Joan was often at the secluded chapel of Bermont. In the quiet places she was being instructed for the great days ahead, trained for a mission such as has never been assigned to another in all the world's history.

She no longer shared the labor of the fields or tended the flocks, and with three brothers for such work there was little need. She had been taught to sew and to spin and at such things became very skillful. There was enough for her to do in the home, and when one thinks of the long days spent with her devout mother Isabelle Romée, the wonder grows that she did not reveal something of the story of her celestial visitors. We have her own word that she did not do this.

Yet she may have let fall something of what was in her mind, for one night her father dreamed that she would "go with the soldiers." Joan's mother told her of this dream, adding that Jacques d'Arc had said to his sons: "If I believed that the thing I dreamed of her would happen I would wish that you might drown her and if you did not do it I would drown her myself." The Voices had been coming to her more than two years at this time so she would be then about fifteen.

It is certain that Joan longed for a confidant and was often on the point of trusting in some friend. To Michel Lebuin, a playmate from childhood, she said: "There is between Coussey and Vaucouleurs a young girl who before another year will cause to be crowned the King of France."

This happened on the eve of Saint John the Baptist, June 23, 1428. Domrémy was between Coussey and Vaucouleurs and the year would only need to stretch into another month to bring fulfillment. A generation earlier a woman known as Marie of Avignon had predicted that France, ruined by a woman, would be saved by a maid from the borders of Lorraine. Joan had heard this prophecy. France had been ruined by the King's unworthy mother, Isabeau of Bavaria; Domrémy was on the borders of Lorraine; Joan's Voices had told her that she herself was the maid who would lift up the fallen kingdom.

"Comrade, if you were not a Burgundian, I would tell you something," she one day said to another friend, a man considerably older than herself. Her friend imagined that she wished to tell him of some offer of marriage that had been made to her. She had called him "Burgundian," but he could not have been very fiercely of that party. At a later day Joan said that there had been in Domrémy but one Burgundian whose head she wished might have been cut off—quickly adding, "providing it was pleasing to God." This could hardly have been her comrade.

Joan was now sixteen, a marriageable age for a girl of that

day, so that her friend's conclusion was fair enough. As to her appearance, we know little more than that she was strong, of good height and carriage, and we have the words of one who was nearest her during her days of battle that she was "beautiful and well formed."[1] We may picture her as wearing the bodice and red wool skirt of the peasant girl of her day, her hair loose or braided, her feet in *sabots*, in summer bare. She wore no ornaments except two small cheap rings given her by her parents and one of her brothers. One of the rings had on it three crosses and the words "JESUS MARIA." Such rings were not uncommon but hers she held as very sacred, for they had been on her hands when she embraced the saints and so were consecrated.

1. "Belle et bien formée." Testimony of Jean d'Aulon, chief of Joan's personal staff.

III

THE VOICES OBEYED

A dark hour for France

      The long-dreaded raid of the Burgundians came to Domrémy that year. In July 1428 the enemy swept in from the westward with fire and sword. What happened to the other villages is not told, but one morning the alarm ran through the streets of Domrémy, the bells rang, the villagers wildly bundled their possessions into carts and with their flocks went helter-skelter down the road toward Neufchâteau, a fortified town. The warning had been in time and they got safely away with their chief possessions. A good many of the fugitives put up at an inn kept by a worthy woman called "La Rousse," from her ruddy hair. In that day when surnames were few such nick-names were much the fashion.

    Joan, strong and willing, assisted La Rousse with her household labors, heavier than usual with a whole village as guests.

Within a week, however, word came that the raiders were gone, after burning or partly burning the village in revenge for its lack of spoil. The villagers returned to find their homes in a state of havoc, their little church so damaged by fire that the people of Domrémy for a time attended the church of the adjoining village of Greux.

But now came news of greater and graver events. The English having conquered northern France were rapidly moving southward, occupying towns, plundering right and left. Jargeau, Meung, Beaugency on the river Loire were taken. Worse than this, the great city of Orléans was besieged. It was the twelfth of October that the siege had begun; it may have been a fortnight later when the report reached Domrémy.

It was a dark hour for France. Orléans was the key to the country below the Loire; if the English captured it France would be no longer France but a chattel of England—it was little more than that already. As for Charles VII, he would end his days in exile, probably in Scotland or Spain.

Joan's Voices now became very urgent. We have her own statement that two or three times a week they exhorted her to go to France.

"The Voice kept urging me—I could no longer endure it. It told me that I would raise the siege of Orléans, it told me to go to Robert de Baudricourt, captain, and that he would give me men; for I was a poor girl, knowing neither how to ride nor to conduct war."

Joan was face to face with the work she had to do. Until now it had seemed hazy and far-off—something for the future, never quite to be met as a reality. Now she must act. The thought dazed her.

Her parents must not know. Jacques d'Arc would promptly deprive her of her liberty; he might even make good his threat of two years before and so put an end to her mission before it had begun. Yet it was necessary to speak to somebody—one who could make even a beginning possible. The young girl was torn with emotions; she had never disobeyed her parents, now she was planning to mislead them.

Of this she said: "Since God had commanded it it was right to do it." She added that if she had been a daughter of a king, still would she have gone. She said that her Voice had been willing that she should tell her parents, except for the sorrow they would have caused her. Her Voice had left it to her to tell her father and her mother or to keep silent. We feel something of the struggle behind these words.

She finally turned to one as humble as herself, a peasant, Durand Laxart of Burey, a village near Vaucouleurs. Laxart had married her mother's cousin and as he was much older than herself, Joan called him "Uncle." She somehow got word to the Laxart home that she wished to see him. When Laxart arrived she begged of him to ask her parents that she might be allowed to go home with him to care for his wife, then in delicate health. Knowing nothing of her real purpose this good soul agreed. The consent of her parents obtained, Joan, with her uncle, set out on her great mission.

There is a question as to the time of their going but it must have been somewhat after the news of the siege of Orléans. There are good reasons for believing that it was near the end of December 1428, within a week or two of Joan's seventeenth birthday. As to their mode of travel, it is likely that they walked; also, that they set out early, for the distance to Burey was considerable. Of those who testified later only three recalled having seen them go: little Mengette, to whom Joan had said: "Adieu, Mengette, I commend thee to God," and Jean Waterin and Gérard Guillemette, who saw them pass through Greux and heard Joan say adieu to the people there.

But to little Hauviette, la préférée, she had sent no word of her going; perhaps she could not.

"I did not know that she had gone," Hauviette said, telling of it long after, "and I wept bitterly. She was so good and I loved her so much. She was my friend."

France owes a debt of gratitude to Durand Laxart

Leaving Greux behind them Joan and Uncle Laxart took the road that follows the Meuse—a road frozen and rough at that season. It is a strange picture when we think of it—those two peasants, as humble as any to be found in France, the man in a wool cap and jerkin; the girl wearing a hood, some sort of cape, a worn and patched red skirt, both of them in *sabots*, setting out on a winter's day to lift up a fallen kingdom. Durand Laxart was ignorant of his part in the mission until they got well beyond the village. Then Joan said: "I must tell you something. I wish to go to France—to the Dauphin, to have him crowned."

The people of Domrémy always spoke of "going to France" as if it were a separate country. Honest Durand Laxart would seem to have been too startled to reply. He knew Joan's earnest and devout nature and that she spoke seriously. Then immediately she added: "Has it not already been said that France would be desolated by a woman and must be restored by a maid? I want you to go and tell Sire Robert de Baudricourt to have me conducted to where my lord the Dauphin is."

Very likely Durand Laxart had never in his life spoken a word to Robert de Baudricourt. He had watched that burly captain ride by at the head of his bristling guard and he may now have dimly wondered how long a peasant like himself would last after entering the grim presence on such an errand. Yet he seems not to have hesitated. Whether or not he believed in the prophecy, he believed in Joan. His reply to her is lost, but he took her at once to Vaucouleurs. The nation of France owes a debt of gratitude to Durand Laxart.

Joan faces De Baudricourt

That afternoon, or next morning, Joan and Uncle Laxart toiled up the steep hill to the governor's castle. Unusual visitors in that forbidding place of stone bastions and armed men, they seem to have had little difficulty in obtaining admission to the governor's presence. If Laxart himself made any statement there it has been forgotten. None was needed. Joan from the beginning of her mission never lacked for words, never was awed or embarrassed before any earthly dignity. She said later that she recognized De Baudricourt on seeing him. "My Voices told me it was he." When he brusquely demanded what she wanted, she answered: "I have come to you on the part of my Lord in order that you may send word to the Dauphin to hold fast and not to cease the war against his enemies. Before mid-Lent the Lord will give him help. In truth, the kingdom belongs not to the Dauphin but to my Lord. But my Lord wills that the Dauphin be made King, and have the kingdom in command. Notwithstanding his enemies the Dauphin will be made King, and it is I who will conduct him to the coronation."

De Baudricourt listened to this long speech, half annoyed, half amused. He thought her irresponsible, flighty.

"Who is your Lord?" he demanded.

"The King of Heaven."

The burly governor turned to the anxious Laxart. The girl must be brought to her senses.

"Take her to her father's home and box her ears," he said, and as the couple turned away he more than once repeated: "Take her to her father's home and box her ears."

Some of those who listened, rough guards and men-at-arms, laughed loudly at the governor's verdict. But among them a young squire, Bertrand de Poulengy, was moved by this peasant girl who, unafraid, delivered her message. One might well pledge his sword to such as she. It is from Bertrand de Poulengy that we know today of that first meeting of Joan and De Baudricourt. Only, the gallant squire forgot the governor's order as to Joan's ears. That detail was supplied by Durand Laxart, the only thing he could remember of the meeting.

"To thee, Joan, I pledge my knightly faith"

De Poulengy thought Joan now returned to Domrémy but it is more likely that she went with her uncle to Burey. She would hardly leave her aunt so soon; also, the news of her visit to De Baudricourt would at once travel to Domrémy, making it unwise for her to meet the fury of Jacques d'Arc. She may never have returned to Domrémy at all, though she must have seen her parents again for she once said that they "nearly lost their minds" when she left for Vaucouleurs. This scene could have occurred at the Laxart home in Burey, to which place they would certainly follow her as soon as they heard of her visit to the governor.

They made at least one effort to put an end to her mission. Apparently they did not wish to use force, not in the face of public opinion that almost from the first moment saw in Joan "something divine." They chose a milder and, as they perhaps believed, a surer method. Among the young men of Domrémy willing to marry a handsome, industrious girl like Joan, there was one who made himself believe, or at least made her parents believe, that he had a promise from her. Joan's parents now arranged to have her summoned before the Bishop of Toul in the hope that he would compel fulfillment. The devout Joan would obey a summons from a bishop and there was a fair chance that she would lose the case. Besides, Toul was a good way off, in a hostile country. This would mean delay, and in the meantime . . .

In the meantime Joan had met with another refusal from De Baudricourt and becoming exasperated had declared she would go to Chinon alone, on foot. She would dress as a man, she said, and borrowed a suit of clothes from her uncle. But Laxart would not let her go alone and with a friend of the family, Jacques Alain, set out in her company. They did not go far, only to the little village of St.-Nicolas, a few miles to the southwestward.

"It is not honest," she said, "to go like this," and they returned to Vaucouleurs. Here she found the summons from the Bishop of Toul; also one from the Duke of Lorraine, who had heard of her and, believing her to be a healer and a fortune teller, requested that she come to Nancy. With the duke's message was a safe-conduct, a document which would protect her from Burgundian attack.

Joan was quite willing to go to Nancy. Toul was on the way there; she could stop and defend herself against the charge of having broken her promise. Also, the Duke of Lorraine was rich and powerful and was connected by marriage with the Dauphin of France. There was a chance that she might win him to her cause.

It was just at this moment that another important event occurred—her first meeting with the knight Jean de Novelompont, called Jean de Metz. Wherever Joan went now she was followed by those who believed in her or were curious and one day there stepped forward a young cavalier who said to her: "My child, what are you doing here? Must the King be driven from his kingdom and we become English?"

De Metz said afterward that Joan's dress was "poor and worn and of a red color." Perhaps he spoke to her only out of sympathy or it may be that the "something divine" which so many saw in her had stirred his faith. Joan, he said, answered him: "I have come to this loyal city to speak to Sire de Baudricourt in order that he may conduct me or have me conducted to the King. But he cares neither for me nor my words. Nevertheless before the coming of mid-Lent I must be with the King, even if I must wear my legs down to my knees; for nobody in the world can recover the kingdom of France—save only myself, though I would like better to spin by the side of my poor mother, seeing that this is not my station. Yet I must needs go and I will do this because my Lord wills it so."

Like De Baudricourt, De Metz asked: "Who is your Lord?"

"It is God."

Taking her hands the young cavalier looked into her eyes, saying: "To thee, Joan, I, Jean de Novelompont, called Jean de Metz, pledge my knightly faith, and promise thee, God aiding, that I will conduct thee to the King!"

Gallant Jean de Metz! In all knightly romance there is no finer picture.

"And when do you wish to start?" he asked her.

"Rather today than tomorrow, and tomorrow than afterward."

"And you will take the road in woman's garments!"

"I will willingly take the dress of a man."

She told him, however, that she must first go to Toul and Nancy. It was thirty miles to Nancy and Joan and her uncle somehow obtained horses for the journey. Jean de Metz rode with them as far as Toul, where Joan appeared before the bishop and swore to tell the truth. Being, as she was, a reputed messenger of God with a worthy relative and a knight of degree on her way to hold converse with the Duke of Lorraine, gave Joan a standing in the eyes of the bishop. Looking into her clear countenance and hearing her bravely spoken words he released her from the charge against her and gave her his blessing.

Arriving at Nancy, Joan appeared in the presence of the duke, who told her he wished to consult her about his health. Joan told him that she knew nothing of such things and asked him to give her his son (meaning his son-in-law, René of Anjou, brother of the Queen of France) with men, to accompany her to Chinon. "I will pray God to give you health," she said.

The duke's sympathies were Burgundian and he would make

her no promises, but he gave her a present of four francs, then not so small a sum, equal to nearly one hundred dollars[1] today.

"It is for this that I was born!"

Returning to Vaucouleurs, Joan was now for the most part at the home of Henri and Catherine Royer, where she would be near the castle if summoned. The governor, as she believed, had sent word of her to the King and at any time a messenger might arrive. Meantime, she busied herself with spinning and other duties to offset her keep. With Madame Royer she went to church and to confession. In a vault below the castle was a chapel where she sometimes retired to pray.

It was now the middle of February. The Battle of Rouvray, another French disaster known also as the "Battle of the Herrings," was fought on the twelfth of that month but news of it would take a good ten days to get to Vaucouleurs. There is a legend that Joan told De Baudricourt of this defeat on the day of its occurrence, and that when report of it came he believed in her; but as no mention of such an incident was ever made by those nearest Joan, nor by anyone until thirty-eight years later, this is probably an invention.

De Baudricourt, in fact, seems never to have fully been convinced of Joan's mission. That Jean de Metz and Bertrand de Poulengy believed in her was much in her favor. De Metz had openly pledged himself to take her to the King and De Poulengy as well. These two were going with or without De Baudricourt's sanction. The governor was worried. A time had come when he wished neither to deny Joan nor to become her champion. He had written to the King of her and he may have received an answer. Certain it is that a messenger arrived from Chinon, and whether or not he brought word concerning Joan he did

---

1. Dollar equivalents throughout the text have been changed from the author's original figures to reflect the value of the dollar in the mid-twentieth century. [*ed.*]

bring word of the disaster of the Herrings at Rouvray. Matters were going from bad to worse. It was a time to grasp at straws.

Madame Royer and Joan, spinning most likely, were one day astonished to see approaching the warlike De Baudricourt with the priest whom they knew. The callers entered and took Joan aside. The priest had brought his holy vestments, and putting them on said solemnly to Joan: "If thou art evil, depart from us; if thou art good, approach."

Joan knelt, dragged herself to his knees and remained there; after which governor and priest went away, apparently satisfied. But Joan said to Madame Royer: "It was not well of the priest to do that. He knows me and has heard me in confession."

If this incident happened on the arrival of the news of Rouvray it would be about February 22. Whether Joan had already told of that battle would make little difference. The governor in any case would wish to satisfy himself that she was not a witch. Joan later said that the third time she asked De Baudricourt for help she received it. She probably asked the morning following his visit and set out the same evening. Permission once granted, there must be no delay in starting; the Anglo-Burgundians could get the news and be lying in wait a stone's throw beyond the castle walls.

De Baudricourt was willing enough to be rid of Joan and he really gave her very little besides a sword and his blessing. Those two high-hearted soldiers of fortune, Jean de Metz and Bertrand de Poulengy, belonged to nobody, were under no orders but their own. Colet de Vienne, the King's messenger, and his comrade Richard the Archer were due to go back to Chinon anyway. De Metz and De Poulengy provided funds for the expedition, the citizens of Vaucouleurs presented Joan with suitable clothing (a page's costume) and it was Uncle Laxart and his friend Jacques Alain who furnished her with a horse. Said Laxart: "At the same time Alain of Vaucouleurs and I bought her a horse costing twelve francs for which we assumed the debt."

They bought it on credit, these two good souls, for twelve francs, in that time and place an average price, about equal to three hundred dollars today. They pledged themselves in that amount, which is more than can be said for De Baudricourt, who in all ways seems to have been a prudent person. He made Joan's companions swear to "well and safely conduct her," which cost him nothing, and he gave her a sword from those about the castle. It was as if he had said: "You have made two converts and Colet and Richard are going your way. Here is a sword, and my permission to use it."

Perhaps it is fair to allow that he did give her Colet and Richard, who for the time at least were under his orders; and to add that later, when the expedition had turned out well, he paid the twelve francs for Joan's horse, probably out of the King's funds. That there are certain amusing aspects to this splendid adventure must be confessed, and nobody would appreciate them more than Joan, who was by no means lacking in humor.

It was on the evening of February 3, 1429, that the Maid, as people now called her, with her little army of six—her two knights, their two servants, and the King's messengers—assembled, mounted, in the castle courtyard at the gate opening to the westward, the "Port of France." They must travel by night if they would avoid capture. A group had assembled to see them go and when the portcullis was raised and Joan between her knights was about to pass, a woman called to her: "How can you make such a journey when on all sides are soldiers?"

Joan answered: "I do not fear the soldiers for my road is made open to me; and if the soldiers come I have God, my Lord, who will know how to clear the route that leads to messire the Dauphin. It is for this that I was born."

And as they rode through the stone archway, Robert de Baudricourt called out: "Go, and let come what may!"

After which they passed into the mist and winter gloaming and were lost among the trees, taking the direction of Chinon.

IV

JOAN RIDES TO THE KING

Icy rivers forded in the dark

Joan, between her two cavaliers, followed by their two servants and the King's messengers, completed an army as picturesque as it was small.

"I was clad as a man," Joan said, describing her departure, "wearing a sword which the captain had given me, without other arms." She further said she had taken male dress by command of God and the angels.

Dressed as a youth of the period, mounted and wearing a sword, the young girl made a striking figure. Her hair was cropped and she wore the loose black cap of a page. Her short coat was a kind of tunic belted at the waist. Underneath it was a *justaucorps*, or doublet, a kind of heavy shirt to which the band of her close-fitting leggings was attached by means of "laces and points"—that is to say, stout hooks and a leather thong. High-laced boots or gaiters, spurs and a cape completed her costume. She was seventeen, doing what girls of all ages have dreamed, riding at glorious venture, a knight and a squire on either hand. To her the dream had come true.

Of their winter's journey through the long stretch of forest and desolated field that lay betwen Vaucouleurs and Chinon, little is left to us. The story, if we knew the details, would of itself make an exciting book. Because of the enemy, the "army" must avoid the roads and bridges. Icy rivers, swollen by winter rains, must be forded in the dark. There were four of these between Vaucouleurs and St.-Urbain, their first stop—two of them deep and swift. Joan had ridden as any other peasant child might ride to and from the field. To swim a horse through a racing current was another matter. Without doubt her knights kept her between them. None of them later spoke of this—such things became too common.

It was near morning when they reached the Abbey of St.-Urbain, thirty miles from Vaucouleurs. How grateful was the welcome it offered, the comfort they found within. The distance still to be traveled was more than three hundred miles. Everywhere was the enemy; such roads as there were they could not follow, but must keep to the forest. After St.-Urbain there would be no such protecting shelter. How precious are the brief accounts left by Joan's cavaliers of that terrific winter journey. Said Jean de Metz: "We traveled by night through fear of the English and Burgundians who were in possession of the roads. We were on the road the space of eleven days, always riding."

Always riding, through the winter night and storm, with every little way a black, boiling river and none that by any chance ran in their direction. Sometimes in deep anxiety De Metz said to Joan: "Will you surely do what you say?"

To which she never failed to reply: "Have no fear; what I do I do by commandment."

When they could travel no more they sought out some hidden place to sleep, stretched themselves out in their wet clothing, Joan between her two knights, her sworn protectors from evil. De Metz and De Poulengy both told of this and the latter added: "During the eleven days that our journey lasted we had many afflictions, but Joan always said to us: 'Fear nothing. You shall see how at Chinon the noble Dauphin will greet us with a glad face.' In hearing her speak I felt myself deeply stirred."

Few episodes in knightly annals can compare with the eleven days' journey of this little army, struggling through seemingly endless nights, beset by hidden dangers, dropping down exhausted for a little rest on the frozen ground. A girl of seventeen fording rivers in February and sleeping on the ground afterward! But Joan was strong of body and made stronger by her purpose. Between her faithful knights she probably slept untroubled by doubts and dreams. If only De Poulengy had told us something more of the "many afflictions." Were they night alarms, hairbreadth escapes, accidents, periods of hunger? The country was stripped, picked clean by war; villages were desolated, peasants lying dead at their thresholds. De Metz told of providing Joan with money for alms, without doubt for straggling survivors. Supplies could be found only in the larger places and these were in enemy hands. The King's messengers knew the route and its resources, but two men foraging for themselves is one thing, while provisioning an army of seven is quite another.

Joan herself dismissed this terrific journey with a word. It was her habit to meet troubles without fear and once they were over to put them behind her. "My Voices often came to me," she said. She further said they passed by Auxerre and that she heard mass there at the cathedral. How did she manage this? Auxerre was a hostile city, walled, its massive gates guarded. De Poulengy did not hear mass on the way but De Metz heard it twice. So it was Joan and De Metz who left their camp disguised, crossed the river Yonne, climbed the steep hill, took their chances with the guards at the city gates and threaded their way through the narrow streets to the great cathedral where today there is a statue of the Maid kneeling, with an inscription which tells us that Joan of Arc on her way to Chinon stopped there, February 27, 1429, to pray.

They had been four days coming from Vaucouleurs, a distance, as they traveled, of one hundred and fifty miles. The way to Chinon was longer than that behind them but the worst was over. Another two days of blind paths and dark rivers and they would reach Gien, a friendly city on the Loire. There were marauding bands beyond Gien but the land was loyal and they need not avoid the towns.

Came to Ste.-Catherine-de-Fierbois

At Gien they told who they were and were given welcome. The messengers, possibly the knights, were known there and word quickly flew in every direction that a maid from the borders of Lorraine, fulfilling an old prophecy, was on her way to restore the King. It reached the people shut up in Orléans and gave them hope. It found its way to the besieging English camps and filled them with dread. Captains and men jeered at the idea, but they were afraid. They believed Joan a witch. Of the French army they had no fear; witchcraft was another matter.

Joan did not linger at Gien. She had great work to do—the greatest ever given to one of her years—she must be on her way. Crossing the Loire she may have been reminded that forty miles farther down its waters washed the walls of Orléans, to whose relief she was marching. For the present they must avoid that city, passing below and beyond it.

The season was less bitter now; they rode through a fair, level land where one need not always avoid the roads and where rivers ran in the right direction. They made their way to the Cher and followed it to Selles, to which loyal city she was one day to come in her glory, then presently bending southward came to Ste.-Catherine-de-Fierbois, a famous shrine.

Joan had heard of Fierbois, for word of these holy places traveled far. Many knights made pilgrimages to this chapel of Ste.-Catherine to give thanks for preservation from great danger and to leave some portion of their arms as an offering. Joan had been preserved through great dangers; Saint Catherine was one of her Voices—she would offer prayers from a grateful heart.

She heard three masses at Fierbois and sent a letter to the King at Chinon, now only eighteen miles distant. In this letter she told him that she had traveled far to reach him and knew many things for his good. Afterward she testified: "It seems to me that I said to him . . . that I would know him among all others."

Joan could neither read nor write, and it is not likely that her knights were much better off. Few in that day had these accomplishments. Some priest of Ste.-Catherine's wrote the letter, of which unfortunately no trace remains today. She expected an answer, for in it she asked the King if she should enter the town where he was. None came. Her letter may never have reached Charles, a weakling surrounded by frivolous or malicious triflers, who would be likely to throw aside such a message.

The little army spent the night at Fierbois and was off next morning for Chinon. Arriving at a point where the grim castle on the heights came into view, the peasant girl of Domrémy must have been deeply moved. The long gray pile of towers and buildings and battlements that crowned the hilltop contained her uncrowned King. Her mission was to restore his realm and place the crown upon his head—she, a young girl, humble, unknown, who had been taught only to sew and to spin at her mother's side. The great stronghold was already ancient—weather-beaten by centuries of storm and battle—a frowning front of masonry, terrifying to a heart less resolute than hers.

Joan once spoke of her arrival at Chinon, but said no more than that she "arrived near the King without interference and lodged first at an inn kept by an honest woman."

V

AT THE COURT
OF CHARLES VII

A committee came down from the castle

       Joan was never one to delay, and a messenger
was promptly sent to the castle asking for an audience. The
King may, or may not, have been told of this request.

  Charles's rule was a mockery, his court a sham. He was the
victim of parasites who were jealous and suspicious of any influence from the outside and made it a point to keep from him
anything that might interfere with their pleasure or profit. Chief
among them was Georges de La Trémouille, a greedy traitor
who stopped at no crime which would serve his ends, and
Regnault de Chartres, Archbishop of Reims, who though a
churchman of high rank honored religion only as a form and
had neither charity nor human pity in his heart. These two
dominated Charles and ruled such of his kingdom as remained
to him. The archbishop bore the title of Chancellor and La

Trémouille that of Chief Counselor; Joan's message naturally fell into their hands.

Their first thought was as to how Joan could be used to their own advantage. The King's prestige was waning; La Trémouille, who traded on it with the English and Burgundians, could not afford to see the kingdom of France entirely a ruin, its King in exile. He had read De Baudricourt's letter about Joan and if the girl was what she claimed it seemed worth while to encourage her. On the other hand, she might prove to be a witch and dangerous. Whatever she was she could influence the King against his advisers; one must move cautiously.

So the King's counselors deliberated as to whether he should hear this girl, who came as she said with messages from God. Later in the day a sort of committee came down from the castle to question her.

"Why have you come?" they demanded.

"That I will tell only to the King."

"But it is in the name of the King that you are asked this question."

Joan then answered: "I have been commanded to do two things on the part of the King of Heaven: one, to raise the siege of Orléans; the other, to conduct the King to Reims for sacrament and his coronation."

The committee returned and the Council debated. Some were in favor of letting the King see Joan, others not. The matter had been noised through the castle by this time, arousing the interest and curiosity of the courtiers. Many of the idlers, wishing to see this strange girl who claimed to be sent from God, were in favor of her coming. Furthermore, not all of those about the King were evil. Some, like the King's secretary Alain Chartier, a gentle poet, were stirred by sympathy for the maid; likewise the Queen, Marie of Anjou, and her mother, Yolande of Aragon, Queen of Sicily, two good women, were favorable to Joan from the beginning.

The timid King, by this time aware of what was going on,

asked that this girl, before he saw her, be questioned by men of the Church. Messengers claiming to be sent by Heaven with revelations and warnings were not uncommon. She was probably no more than a fortuneteller. She might even be a witch. Nevertheless, if the priests found her harmless he would see her.

Charles was in the depths of despair. The month following the Battle of Rouvray had been his darkest hour. Poor in spirit and purse, surrounded by his tawdry, time-serving court, he had become childish and querulous. How could he guess that to a little girl dreaming over her spinning he had seemed all that was fine and noble—that listening to illumined beings she had come with messages that would lift him up and give him back his kingdom?

"I am come, being sent on the part of God"

The group of priests who called upon Joan must have found her answers satisfactory for she was told that the King would receive her that same evening—this being the day of her arrival at Chinon. Yet in the very moment of her coming the irresolute Charles, prompted by certain of his counselors, would have sent her away. He was reminded—perhaps by Queens Marie and Yolande—that this girl, commended to him by De Baudricourt, had been conducted across provinces occupied by the enemy and had miraculously forded rivers, to come to him. On this he consented to see her.

Being early March (the sixth), it was dark "after dinner" when, by Joan's statement, she went to the castle. One may picture her with her two knights, mounted, preceded by torches, climbing the steep, stony way that winds up to the entrance, crossing the drawbridge and passing under the arch of the lofty *tour de l'Horloge*, a clock-tower to this day. A space of court to cross, a stair to mount, then a blaze of light, a dazzle of silk and cloth of gold and facing it all a peasant girl who claimed to have brought messages to the King.

At the farther end of the room a fire was roaring up the great chimney. Also, according to Joan, there were "fifty flambeaux and three hundred men at arms." At all events there was a great assembly of both men and women. Any diversion was welcome; a novelty like Joan would bring out every member of the castle.

There was a moment of expectant silence. Those idle, simpering people were curious to see how she looked, what she would do first. What they saw was a lithe, rather slender, fairly tall youth, with cropped hair—Joan in the page's costume she had worn from Vaucouleurs, the suit in which she had forded rivers and slept on the frozen ground; surely a curious figure before that tinsel throng.

If they had expected her to be dazed and awed they were quickly undeceived. Led forward by the Count of Vendôme, what she did was to go immediately to Charles, who occupied no special place but had "retired behind some others," and falling on her knees make him reverence, saying: "Very illustrious Lord Dauphin, I am come, being sent on the part of God, to give succor to the kingdom and to you."

Joan never revealed by what sign she knew the King. Her statement: "I recognized him by the counsel and revelation of my Voice," is as far as she ever went on the subject.

The King led her apart—perhaps to the small tower embrasure at the left of the fireplace where they spoke together. Making reverence, Joan said: "Noble King, I am called Joan the Maid and I tell thee on the part of Messire [God] that thou art the true heritor of France, son of the King, and He sends me to conduct thee to Reims in order that thou receivest there thy coronation and thy sacrament, if such be thy wish."

Charles asked her: "How am I to know that you come from God?" Joan's answer to this was another secret that died with

her; but long after, the King himself, near death, declared that a
little before Joan's coming he had made a secret prayer of which
no one else could know. He had prayed, he said, that if he was
the true heir to the kingdom God would defend him or at the
least grant him the grace to escape without death or prison, allowing him to take refuge in Spain or Scotland, ancient brothers-
in-arms, allies of the kings of France. Joan, the King said,
repeated to him this prayer known only to himself and God,
thus gaining his confidence.

Joan and Charles now returning to the others, all saw the joy
in the King's face. The poet-secretary Alain Chartier wrote:
"It was most manifest the King was greatly encouraged as if
by the Spirit."

Joan's own story of the royal audience was no more than
a few words: "When I entered the presence of the King I
recognized him by the revelation and counsel of my Voices.
I told him I wanted to make war on the English." That was
all; she had arrived "without interference"; the long days and
longer nights were behind her. She told the King she wanted
to make war on the English. It was as when on the road to
Burey she had said to Durand Laxart that she wanted him to
tell Sire Robert de Baudricourt to have her taken to the King.
That was Joan's simple and direct way. She had no use for the
roundabout. She traveled in a straight line to the point in view.

VI

JOAN BEFORE THE WISE MEN

"My cousin, the Duke of Alençon"

        The King had accepted Joan or was about to do so; and that night or very soon after she was given lodging in the tower of Coudray, across a deep ravine but connected by a footbridge with the main castle. The Maid was confided to the care of Madame Bellier, wife of the King's major-domo, with Louis de Contes, a boy of fifteen, named as her page. Her faithful knights remained her special guards.

    The tower of Coudray was very ancient, the largest of a group that really constituted a castle separate from that of the King. Her apartment, a story above the ground, was a large circular room provided with the comforts customary to that day—a few pieces of furniture, skins or rushes on the stone floor, something in the nature of hangings on the wall. There was at least one window, a narrow opening in masonry many feet thick —so thick that at one side it enclosed the staircase—and there was an ample fireplace. To Joan, after her bitter winter journey, all this was luxury.

The fame of her coming and the impression she had made on the King went speeding through the night and the Maid soon found use for her page. Day brought many who wished to see her—nobles from the town and the near-by castles. Among those first to arrive was one who would play a large part in her military fortunes, John, Duke of Alençon. The King's cousin, he was of a race of soldiers. Ancestors of his had died on the fields of Crécy and Agincourt; the young duke himself, made prisoner at the Battle of Verneuil, had spent five years in the fortress of Le Crotoy rather than accept liberty without ransom on condition that he would desert the cause of France. Alençon had been shooting quail on the marshes of St.-Florent, twenty miles west of Chinon, when one of his courtiers came dashing up.

"Great news, Your Highness!" he said. "There has arrived in the King's presence a young girl who declares herself to be sent from God to put the English to flight and raise the siege of Orléans. The King has received her, and she is now lodged in the castle of Coudray!"

Alençon waited to hear no more. If the King had received this girl it was with the sanction of his council. The young duke was off next morning for Chinon, where he found Joan and the King together.

"Who is this?" Joan asked as he approached.

"This," replied the King, "is my cousin, the Duke of Alençon."

"You are very welcome," Joan said. "The more we can get together of the blood of the King of France, the better it will be."

Next day after the King's mass Charles, Joan, Alençon and La Trémouille assembled privately. Addressing the King, Joan made several solemn requests, assuring him that if these were complied with God would restore him to the estate of his fathers. Later, lance in hand and mounted, she rode in the presence of the King and Alençon. Surprised at her skill, Alençon made her a present of a horse. The duke was a judge of such things. It is easy to believe that riding to Chinon had made Joan a master of horsemanship but on that swift journey who had taught her the manual of the lance?

If Joan now believed that her troubles were over, that she would presently set out at the head of an army to raise the siege of Orléans in the simple, direct manner she pictured so clearly, she was to be sadly disappointed. The King or his counselors decided that the Maid from Lorraine must be further questioned by learned men of the Church. This wonder-working girl might be all that she claimed; then again she might very well be a witch, in league with demons. On the whole, such an inquiry was proper enough; we cannot too often remember the ignorance and super- stition of that day.

The examination troubled Joan less than the delay. She was eager to be at her work, knowing her time for it was to be brief.

"I will last but a year, not much more," she told Alençon, "and I must work well during that year. I have four things to do: to raise the siege of Orléans, to put the English to flight, to have the King crowned at Reims and to deliver the Duke of Orléans from the hands of the English."

Hearing her speak in this way, some thought she prophesied her death. Joan herself did not know what she meant, but only that another year would end her period of usefulness. She did not always speak of the rescue of the Duke of Orléans as a part of her mission though she always so regarded it. Next to the King, her heart went out to Duke Charles, the poet, held a pris- oner in England. It was natural that she would mention this to Alençon, for he had married the duke's daughter.

Joan in her tower

Confronted by the learned doctors, Joan was asked: "Why have you come, and who sent you to the King?"

And, as always, she replied: "I came on the part of the King of Heaven. I have Voices and a Council that tell me what to do." Alençon, who was present, could remember no more of the examination than this. There was really no more to remember; whatever the details of the answers this was their sum and substance. Joan, a peasant girl, before a great array of priests, it was a picture that time would make only too familiar. Her page, Louis de Contes, who was much with her in the tower of Coudray, often saw her on her knees. She was seeking wisdom and guidance in her answers. He remembered that she wept.

He saw her go to and from "the house of the King," doubtless trying to bestir that dallying monarch, and he announced the persons of great estate who came to confer with her. The Duke of Alençon presently took her for a brief visit to his wife and mother at the Abbey of St.-Florent, a happy relief from the doctors; even from the King, with his sinister counselors. The Alençon ladies made much of Joan during the three or four days of her stay and the latter in good humor and friendship christened Alençon *"mon beau duc,"* afterward calling him only by that name. It is pleasant to remember Joan's visit to St.-Florent, for it was one of the few wholly serene incidents of her brief career.

Also, we like to think of Joan in the quiet of her tower and to picture her sometimes at evening looking out from the battlements on the scene that so long had made the castle of Chinon a favorite residence of kings.

It was one of the fairest views in France: a river that came out of the east and made a path of light across the world; the valley with its level fields and undulating slopes showing here and there a glimpse of the farther blue; the little city just below with its ancient bridge (ancient even then), its battlemented walls, its high, sharp roofs and near and far the feathered poplars and pointed cypresses—in a word, France; the France she had come to save. From infancy the girl had known a picture world such as this and at moments she must have remembered that along the Meuse the hills would soon be turning green.

*"Take me to Orléans and I will show you
signs why I am sent"*

The Chinon examination could have lasted no
more than a few days but to Joan it was long and wearisome.
She told Alençon that though much questioned she had not told
all that she knew and could do. It was over at last but the end
was not yet. After hearing the report of the doctors the King
and his counselors decided that the Maid must go to Poitiers, a
seat of learning, for still another examination. Joan was in despair.

"In God's name," she said, "I well know that I shall have much
to go through at Poitiers! But God will aid me. Now let us be
going."

So for Poitiers Joan set out, accompanied by the King and the
two Queens, with many fine lords and ladies, the poet-secretary
Alain Chartier and of course the Archbishop of Reims and La
Trémouille, who never would let Joan and the King out of their
sight together. Joan's two knights also rode with her, and her
little page, Louis de Contes. Altogether, a goodly escort for a
peasant girl from the banks of the Meuse. In this fine company
she appeared as a handsome youth, for there is no reason to
suppose that she had changed the form of her dress though
certainly now it would be of a more seemly cut and of finer
material; Marie of Anjou and Yolande of Aragon had looked
to that.

It was on the sixth of March that Joan arrived at Chinon and
it was during the third week of that same month that this fine
cavalcade set out for the university city of Poitiers, fifty miles
to the southward. The Maid's stay at Coudray had been brief
but much had happened and any new experience seems long.
Now it was behind her: the hard journey to Chinon, her meeting
with the King, the questionings of the priests were a part of the
remote past. She was on her way to face still another test. She
did not question the outcome—she only chafed at the delay.

She was not downhearted—even in the moments of sorest trial

her spirit seldom faltered. In a moment of irritation she was likely
to speak out sharply but she was naturally cheerful, full of hearty
good humor. To all appearances she rode along as gaily as any
of that careless company.

They stopped one night on the way at one of the great castles
and next day at Poitiers found lodging for the Maid in the home
of Jean Rabateau, King's Advocate in Parliament. Joan's fame
had traveled far, her arrival was a great event. Persons of all ranks
came flocking to see her; the little street in front of the Rabateau
home was thronged with men and women eager for a glimpse
of the girl from Lorraine whom God had sent to restore France.
A little way down the street was the great cathedral, in front of
it a broad, open space where the crowds collected to watch the
Maid pass by to prayer.

Joan's examinations began at once in the Rabateau home. Of
those who attended four lived to tell of them, so we know pretty
well what happened. One of these, Brother Seguin of Seguin, a
man of sour countenance and sharp speech but kind of heart, told
later how Joan became annoyed at what to her seemed pointless
questions. One of the doctors said: "According to your statements the Voice told you that God wished to deliver the people
of France from their present calamities. But if God wishes to
deliver the people of France it is not necessary to have soldiers."

"In God's name," replied Joan, "the soldiers will do battle and
God will give the victory."

Brother Seguin said the questioner was pleased with this answer.
It was now his own turn to question the Maid. Being of the
province of Limousin, Brother Seguin spoke the French of that
region, strange in accent to Joan, whose speech was of the sort
spoken along the Meuse. When he asked sharply: "What dialect
do your Voices speak?" Joan answered: "A better than yours,"
which even Brother Seguin found amusing.

"Do you believe in God?"

"Yes, better than you"; meaning perhaps that her faith was
founded on surer evidence.

"But after all," pursued Brother Seguin sternly, "God does

not wish us to accept you without some sign showing that you must be believed. We shall not be able to counsel the King, on a simple assertion, to confide in you and put in peril the men-at-arms. Have you nothing else to say?"

"I did not come to Poitiers to work signs!" exploded Joan. "But take me to Orléans and I will show you signs why I am sent. Give me men in whatever number shall be judged good, and I will go to Orléans!"

With all his sour manner Brother Seguin liked Joan. None could doubt her honesty or the deep sagacity of her answers, some of which seemed inspired. One of those present said later that Joan replied "as a fine scholar might have done," and that the doctors found in her the "something divine" which so many others saw and felt. The King's poet-secretary Alain Chartier wrote: "Marvelous spectacle! woman among men; unlearned among doctors, she disputed, she so little, on the highest questions." Marvelous indeed it was, and the more so when we reflect that this "woman" was a girl of seventeen.

Joan's impatience with men of words, her eagerness for men of action, came out one day when a vigorous young squire who had ridden with the King's party from Chinon appeared in the Rabateau home. The Maid had found in him a congenial companion and now gave him a hearty welcome. Striking him on the shoulder, she said: "I would like well to have many men of such good will!"

The doctors assembling, one of them began: "We are sent to you on the part of the King . . ."

"I can well believe," Joan broke in, "that you are sent to question me. I do not know *A* from *B*."

"Why, then, have you come?"

"I have come on the part of the King of Heaven to raise the siege of Orléans and to conduct the King to Reims that he may be crowned and anointed. Have you paper and ink, master Jean Erault? Write what I am going to say," and forthwith the eager girl began her first summons to the English: "*You, Suffolk, Glas-*

dale and La Pole, I summon you on the part of the King of the Heaven to return to England!"

No more than this beginning was dictated at the moment but a complete letter was written very soon after, March 22, when Joan had been in Poitiers no more than three or four days. In its completed form it began:

✠ JESUS MARY ✠

King of England, and you, Duke of Bedford, who call yourself Regent of the kingdom of France; you, William de la Pole, Count of Suffolk; John, Lord Talbot; and you, Thomas, Lord of Scales, who call yourselves lieutenants of the said Duke of Bedford, do justly by the King of Heaven; render to the Maid who is sent here by God, the King of Heaven, the keys of all the good cities you have taken and violated in France. She has come here from God to restore the royal blood. She is all ready to make peace, if you will deal rightfully by her, acknowledge the wrong done France, and pay for what you have taken.

Proceeding, her letter warned the soldiers, nobles and others to leave Orléans and go back to their own country, thus saving their lives. She had been sent, she said, to put them one and all out of France, which God intended King Charles to rule. And if they did not go her army would "strike in their midst," making a commotion such as had not been known in France for a thousand years. God would give her strength, she said, to do these things. She ended by inviting the English Regent, Duke of Bedford, to join in doing a great deed for Christianity (meaning a crusade against unbelievers), closing with a final warning that if he did not make peace at Orléans he would shortly have reason to remember it to his great sorrow.

In this letter Joan is named as *chef de guerre*, war chief. At a later time she said she had not dictated these words, which is not important, for even if the words were supplied by her secretary they show that by March 22, a few days after her arrival, she had won or was about to win her case. Joan's letter is that of one unskilled in the art of fine words, but with something to say and fiercely moved from within. As always, she scorned the roundabout, going straight to the mark as best she knew how.

The examination ended by the doctors holding a general meeting where it was concluded that as nothing evil had been found in her but only evidence of good faith, the King could properly accept her aid and provide her with soldiers with which to go to Orléans against the besiegers. It has been said that the King sent to Domrémy to make inquiry there about Joan, but this is unlikely. In her two knights he had good witnesses, and he had received word of her from De Baudricourt. Nor had there been time for a commission to reach Domrémy, make inquiries there and return to Poitiers. The learned doctors accepted Joan on her own statements and the clear-eyed sincerity behind them. They had never seen her like—one so direct, fearless, simple of speech. Asked why she called the King "Dauphin," she answered: "I will not call him King until he shall have been crowned and anointed at Reims. It is to that city that I intend to lead him."

She had no doubts, no hesitations, no ifs. The completeness of her faith inspired faith in her listeners.

The people of Poitiers rejoiced with the Maid in the happy ending of her examinations. During her brief stay her lodgings had been sought by visitors of the highest rank. Now, she was going to lead soldiers to Orléans and give victory to France.

The examiners joined in a written report to the King in which they declared that in Joan had been found only "humility, purity, devotion, honesty, simplicity. . . . The King must not prevent her from going to Orléans with his soldiers but must have her conducted honorably, trusting in God." Many copies of this report were sent, not only throughout France, but to distant lands. Joan's fame ran far and wide. She was called a new Saint Catherine and credited with miracles.

VII

THE MAID PREPARES FOR WAR

The King commands the armor

Charles did not waste time waiting for the written report but at once ordered that soldiers and supplies be collected for the march on Orléans. Queen Yolande, a woman of much ability, went to Tours and Blois to begin preparations, being presently joined by the Duke of Alençon, sent by the King to assist her.

Joan was now in fact *chef de guerre*, chief of war. It was the royal decree that captains and all others of whatever rank must follow her leadership. Those hardened old warriors—many of them Armagnac raiders and captains of "free companies"—would not always be easy to handle, which is no wonder when we remember that for years they had been little more than bandits, obeying nobody, not even the King. What they really thought of the King's order and of Joan we shall never know. Probably it semed to them a great new adventure, led by a kind of mascot or enchantress who was going to give them victory. Whatever they thought, they began arriving at Tours and were sent on to Blois, where Queen Yolande and Alençon had organized their camp.

Joan with her page had also come to Tours, conducted by Jean d'Aulon, called "one of the best men in the kingdom," named by the King as chief of her personal staff. They rode with Queen Yolande, who provided them with lodgings in the luxurious home of an old friend and former maid of honor, Eleanore de Paul, now married to a distinguished citizen, Jean du Puy.

At Tours it must have seemed to Joan that her troubles had come to an end. The people thronged about her, wearing small medals struck in her honor. Soldiers marched through the streets, her soldiers-to-be, breaking into cheers when she appeared among them. In all this she found a divine assurance of victory. She was humbly grateful for having been chosen to save France.

The Maid's military household received important additions at Tours. A second page, a youth called Raymond, was assigned to her; also a priest, Father Pasquerel, as almoner and confessor. Furthermore, she was joined by two of her brothers, Jean and Pierre, who, hearing the astonishing reports, had followed their sister to war. How proud they were of her and how eagerly she listened to their news! Her devout mother had undertaken a pilgrimage to a distant shrine to pray for her soldier daughter!

The King commanded that armor be constructed for Joan and for each of her brothers. Tours was famous for its armorers —there was a whole street of them—but the master workman to whom was given the task of fashioning a suit of steel for the Maid must have found himself somewhat puzzled. He had never made armor before for a young girl, and to get it gracefully shaped and adjusted and comfortable to the wearer was something of a task.

It was what is known as "white armor," of polished, unbrowned steel and very beautiful. It gave the wearer an unearthly look and probably no one better than Joan realized the effect this would have on her followers and upon the enemy. It was such armor as this that Saint Michael had worn in her visions of him—the armor of the holy pictures, the armor of Heaven.

By an ancient record of the city of Tours Joan's armor cost the sum of one hundred francs, the equal of two thousand dollars today. As we have seen, a strong horse in that day could be had for twelve francs. Joan's armor cost the value of eight horses. Her two knights were likewise provided with new armor. Everywhere was preparation for the great campaign—busy days for the armorers of Tours.

A banner and a sword

Joan still had the sword presented to her by Robert de Baudricourt. She now learned that her heavenly Council wished her to have something different, a blade consecrated by knightly deeds. At Ste.-Catherine-de-Fierbois, the Voices said, there was buried near the altar a sword upon which were stamped five crosses. They told her to send for it.

Joan sent an armorer of Tours with a letter to the clergy at Fierbois, telling them of this and asking them to send the sword provided that it was their wish that she should have it. They searched as she directed and found the sword with the five crosses on it, buried not very deeply in the earth but covered with rust. The priests who reverently undertook to remove the rust reported that it fell away at their touch. Afterward, with those of Tours, they had two sheaths made for it, one of red velvet and one of cloth of gold. But these were not for service. Joan herself had another made, a strong sheath of leather. This sword Joan especially loved. Her Voices had directed her to it and it had been found near the altar of Saint Catherine, one of her Voices. The reader will remember Fierbois as the place of Joan's last stop before Chinon. The sword had belonged to some brave knight—tradition said to Charles Martel, who had offered it on the altar of Saint Catherine after his victory over the Saracens, in 732.

Even more than her sword Joan prized her banner. It was made for her in Tours by commandment, as she said, of Saint Catherine and Saint Margaret. The material of this banner was white linen or fustian and it was fringed with silk. On it was the figure of God holding the world, at each side a kneeling angel. Inscribed upon it were the words JESUS MARIA, and the field of it was "sown with lilies."

Joan also had a pennon on which was pictured the Annunciation, with an angel holding a lily. The work on the banner and on the pennon was done by a man named Hauves Poulvoir who had a daughter named Héliote, of about Joan's age. During the days when the work was in progress Joan and pretty Héliote Poulvoir became close friends. Joan was a soldier getting ready for battle but amid all the warlike preparations she found joy in the friendship of this young girl. It is easy to imagine the awe in which little Héliote would hold the Maid who communed with Voices that were sending her to war.

"Joan, Joan, won't you be afraid when you face the cannons and the arrows and the poised spears?"

"I may be—that is with God. It is certain that I am to be wounded—my blood will flow."

"Joan!"

"Yes, it has been revealed to me."

"And you will still go?"

"I must go, though it be to my death."

We know that Joan at Tours spoke of the wound she would receive at Orléans, for it is mentioned in a letter written a full two weeks before the event. Yet in spite of the prospect of battle and the knowledge that she must suffer, her month there could hardly have been less than a happy one. For the moment she had to face neither conspiracy nor bloodshed. Wherever she turned there was love, faith and friendliness. The blessings of the cathedral were conferred upon her, her banner and her arms. Her lodgings were sought by those who regarded her as the hope of France. She was on the way to do the work for which she was born.

VIII

THE GIRL IN WHITE ARMOR

Joan makes rules of war

One morning—it was the beginning of the last week of April 1429—Joan and her staff crossed the bridge at Tours and turned to the eastward, toward Blois. It was a handsome sight: Joan in glistening armor, with Jean d'Aulon; her two knights, Jean de Metz and Bertrand de Poulengy; her two brothers, Jean and Pierre d'Arc; her two pages, Louis de Contes and Raymond; finally, as a sort of rear guard, Father Pasquerel and Regnault de Chartres, Archbishop of Reims. Riding two by two across the long bridge in the spring morning they made a goodly show and the streets and waterfront of Tours were thronged. There may have followed a body of troops; belated arrivals were always going.

It is thirty-six miles to Blois, a good day's ride. Joan saw little of her army that night—no more than a few of the leaders. From them she learned that there were plenty of soldiers and supplies and did not much concern herself with the problem as to how they had been obtained. What troubled her was the army's morals and behavior. Her captains were an assembly of hard-fighting, hard-drinking, profane, war-worn leaders of Armagnac bands and free companies, men like La Hire, at once the terror and admiration of France, Marshal Giles de Rais, later called "Blue-beard," Ambrose de Loré and others like them—men whose business it was to fight and pillage, leaving morals to the priests. As for the soldiers, probably a more dissolute lot of sinners was never assembled to fight the battles of a fallen nation. A hundred years of war and crime had yielded this human harvest.

The stray glimpses of her army that Joan got on the evening of her arrival gave her a good deal of a shock. Everywhere there was wild drinking, gambling, ribaldry and worse. The streets and wine shops of Blois were filled with reeling, rioting men and women.

The Maid did not hesitate as to what she must do. That night or next morning she assembled her captains and told them that this nightmare of wickedness must end—not gradually but at once. The drinking orgies and profanity must cease; the disso-lute camp followers must go; the men, also the captains, must say their prayers and go to mass and confession if they wished to march under the banner of Heaven.

Those battered chiefs were at first in despair but looking into Joan's earnest face they finally agreed to go to confession and to pray. Even La Hire, whose every other word had been an oath, promised to swear only by his staff. He composed for himself a prayer. It ran: "Oh, God, do with me as I would do by you if you were La Hire and I were God."

The news of Joan's proposed reforms reached the soldiers and the effect may be imagined. Few could have seen her on her arrival the night before and now when the report of her orders flew there was at first astonishment, then roars of laughter. Those crime-soaked children of war could not believe their ears. They had learned to swear as soon as they could talk, debauchery was their only diversion. As for going to confession, why in a month they could not even begin the story of their misdeeds.

But then their captains appeared, La Hire and the others, and riding among them banner in hand, a figure in white armor, straight from a church window or from the gates of paradise. Ribaldry ceased and did not begin again when she had passed. That day and the next she rode among them. Joan had a natural instinct for dramatic effect and consciously or otherwise often followed it. To those awe-stricken soldiers that face of light and that suit of shining armor could belong only to an angel.

Meantime she had told Father Pasquerel to have painted a banner around which to assemble the priests. Upon it was painted the Crucifixion and each day the priests gathered about it, chanting anthems and hymns. Joan was with them but she gave orders that no soldier who had not confessed that day would be allowed to assemble there, and she notified all to confess and come, that they might be purified to march under the banner of God. Father Pasquerel's corps of priests became busy with confessions. The morning and evening assemblies swelled into vast chanting congregations. Such general and immediate reform was never before known.

On the morning of the third day after the Maid's arrival the army made ready to set out for Orléans. Pasquerel assembled the priests; the banner at their head, they opened the march; captains and soldiers followed, and the wagon trains. The great procession crossed the bridge to the south bank of the Loire and, chanting hymns, turned eastward, priests and soldiers singing as they marched. Apart from the Crusades no similar spectacle had been known to history.

The way to Orléans

The Maid kept to no one place in her army but was everywhere among the soldiers, urging them to have faith

and to confess and pray—to them, strange counsel from a commander. That night for the first time she slept in her armor and was much bruised as a result. It was the end of April when nights in that part of France are none too warm. To lie down on the ground in a casing of metal was a sore trial after the luxurious beds of Eleanore de Paul at Tours. Whether she repeated the experiment on the second night we do not know. Later, in the field, it became her custom to sleep in that way.

Joan's army made an imposing spectacle as it wound its way through the springtime along the banks of the Loire: the chanting priests and armored knights, the gleaming lances and ranks of bowmen, the wagon loads of provisions—sixty of them, the herd of more than four hundred cattle. The Maid's soldiers probably numbered not more than four thousand but with that gleaming object riding among them, assuring them of certain victory, they were enough. At evening and at morning an altar was raised in the fields, priests with their pictured standards assembled to intone the service, while all about knelt soldiers who heretofore had known war only as rapine, barbarity and evil living. By the time they reached Orléans the "terrible English hurrah" which alone had been enough to frighten them had lost most of its terrors.

Orléans is thirty-five miles from Blois. The army spent two nights on the way and on the third afternoon arrived opposite the besieged city. Here Joan found herself in a quandary. Either she had believed Orléans to be on the south side of the river or that she would be able to cross before arriving there, for she had expected to march straight into the city past the English forts. There were also some English strongholds on the side of the river where she now found herself—one of them, the fort of St.-Jean-le-Blanc, so near that the English and French could see each other plainly. Disappointed at finding herself across the river from Orléans, Joan was of a mind to march at once on this fort. Persuaded otherwise, she led the army to a point beyond it where some barges were waiting, sent by the people of Orléans to transport the provisions across the river. The siege of Orléans, it should be explained, was not a complete one—the city being not entirely surrounded. French soldiers could and did pass in and out and provisions were sometimes brought in, though always at the risk of capture by the English, who kept watch from their towers and forts.

"Most joyous at her coming"

Joan by this time was angry enough. Her whole plan to march into Orléans, disregarding the English forts, was upset. If her army crossed in the boats, it would be by an almost endless ferrying process to a kind of back-way entrance, humiliating to Joan and heartening to the enemy. Moreover it would be dangerous, for when a part of the army should still be left on the south bank the English from the forts there might easily make a sortie and capture it. Furthermore, the wind was downstream and the barges, even those used to transport the provisions, could by no means get to the point five miles above where it was safe for them to cross.

It was just at this point that Dunois, military commander of Orléans, half brother to Duke Charles of that city, appeared on the scene. Dunois had been greatly interested in the Maid, ever since he had heard the first rumor of her arrival, two months before. He now approached to bid her welcome. Joan was not in a gracious humor and did not waste words. She abruptly demanded if he was Dunois of Orléans. On being told that he was, she said: "Was it you who gave counsel that I come here on this side of the river, and that I am not to go directly where are Talbot and the English?"

Dunois answered: "I and those wiser than I have given this counsel, believing it to be better and safer."

"In God's name," replied Joan, "the counsel of our Lord is safer and wiser than yours. You have thought to deceive me, and you deceive yourself more; for I bring you better help than ever came to any knight or city whatever, seeing that it is from the King of Heaven."

At that moment the wind, which had been contrary and had kept the boats from ascending the river, veered and changed. The sails were spread and they made their way upstream to where the convoy of provisions now waited to be carried over. All regarded this as a miracle; Dunois, who told of it, said: "From this moment I had great confidence in Joan, more than I had until that time."

It is hard today to understand why Joan's captains had let the army come up on the lower side of the river unless they expected Orléans to send boats enough to take it across in a prompt and safe manner. The army could not hope to cross by the bridge, which was in the hands of the English, stoutly fortified and defended. As for the forts on the Orléans side, Joan somehow knew, as her captains seem *not* to have known, that Talbot and his men there, poorly provisioned and already half discouraged as to the outcome of the siege, were not in a fighting mood— that to appear among them suddenly and without fear, with her chanting priests, her white armor and banner of Heaven, her long array of knights and spearmen, her bowmen and wagon trains and herds—her army of God, in a word—would paralyze their energies, render them helpless. She now declared to Dunois that she would march back with her whole army to Blois, cross there and come up on the other side, as first intended.

Dunois pleaded with her not to do this. The people of Orléans, he said, were filled with a great desire to see her. Her appearance among them would inspire them with renewed hope and courage, which they much needed.

"I must stay with my soldiers," said Joan, "now confessed and penitent and of good will. I cannot tell what may happen if they go back without me." Her fear was that having once marched up the river on a fool's errand they would drift away, especially as she knew that some in Blois were unfavorable to the expedition.

But Dunois could not permit Joan to go back. He went hastily to the captains who had marched with her—La Hire and the others—and begged them in the name of the King to prevail upon the Maid to enter Orléans. They must themselves go back with the army to hold it together; also the priests with their banner, to keep it from falling again into evil ways. To this the captains agreed and joined Dunois in pleading with Joan to remain. Consenting, she ordered the army's return to Blois and with a small body of her soldiers crossed the river to Chécy, five miles above Orléans. Here she spent the night and most of the next day while the provisions were being conveyed into the city, where they were much needed. During the day a party of knights and squires came from Orléans to receive her, "most joyous at her coming, all of whom made great reverence and welcome and so she made to them."

This was on the twenty-ninth of April, and it was on that evening that Joan of Arc entered Orléans. The ancient chronicler above quoted—probably himself present—quaintly and beautifully tells the story of her entry:

> Thus at eight o'clock of the evening, notwithstanding all the English who in no wise prevented it, she entered fully armed mounted on a white horse; and borne before her her standard, which was likewise white and had on it two angels holding each a lily flower in her hand. . . .
>
> She thus entering into Orléans had on her left side Dunois, armed and mounted most richly. And after them came several other nobles and valiant lords, squires, captains and soldiers. And was received by other soldiers and burghers and burgesses of Orléans, carrying torches in great number and making such joy as if they saw God descend among them, and not without cause, for they had many wearinesses, hardships and trials; and what was worse, great doubt of succor and fear to lose body and goods. But they felt wholly recomforted and as if freed from siege by the divine virtue which they had been

told was in the simple Maid, whom they regarded most affectionately, men, women and little children.

And there was a most marvelous press to touch her or the horse on which she was. So great was it that one of those who carried the torches approached so near her standard that fire caught the pennon. Whereupon she touched her horse with the spurs and turned him as gracefully to the pennon, of which she extinguished the fire as if she had long followed the wars. And this the soldiers held in great wonder and the burghers of Orléans also, and accompanied her the length of their town and city making most great welcome, and in very great honour conducting her almost to the Regnart gate to the home of Jacques Boucher, then treasurer of the Duke of Orléans, where she was received with great joy, with her two brothers and the two gentlemen and their varlets who had come with her from their country of Barroys.

Meaning, of course, Jean de Metz and De Poulengy—Vaucouleurs and Domrémy being in the old province of Barroys. Another there said that such was the joy of the inhabitants that it seemed as if the young girl was an angel of God. "By means of the Maid," they said, "we are at last going to escape our enemies."

In the home of Jacques Boucher, Joan occupied a room and a bed with little Charlotte Boucher, the treasurer's nine-year-old daughter. Her chief of staff, Jean d'Aulon, and her page, Louis de Contes, were also lodged there. Joan's other page, Raymond, is not again mentioned and seems to have been left at Blois. Long afterward, when little Charlotte Boucher was a woman, she spoke of the Maid's visit, of her simple, religious habits—how before an attack she took communion and heard mass.

"Many times she said to my mother: 'Trust in God. God will aid the city of Orléans and expel the enemy.'"

IX

ORLEANS

The Maid waits for her army

Joan next morning was ready to begin battle with such soldiers as remained in Orléans. Rather unwillingly she allowed herself to be persuaded by Dunois to wait until her own troops returned from Blois. He would go, he said, with certain of his captains, to direct their course back to Orléans. The Maid contented herself with sending a message to Lord Talbot, commander of the English forces, warning him that unless he returned to England his army would be driven out by force. No reply came, but according to Dunois, Joan's letter, "couched in her maternal tongue, and all in very simple words," put fear into the hearts of the English. Two hundred of the English were no longer able to put to flight a thousand of the French, he declared; indeed, it was soon the other way about.

In return the English may have thought to frighten Joan, for during the day they sent word to her that she was nothing but a cowherd and that unless she went back to her cattle they would burn her. In the evening Joan went out on the bridge and called to Glasdale, English commander of the Tourelles (the towers at the farther end), bidding him, in the name of God, to surrender, thus saving the lives of his soldiers. Glasdale and those with him called back insults and again threatened to burn her. But this was bravado. The Maid's letter and her warning had been as effective as a victory. The enemy could insult her but their hearts were dead within them.

Next morning Dunois, D'Aulon and others set out for Blois, Joan with La Hire and a guard of soldiers conducting them through the gates and past the English forts (or bastilles, as they were called), from which not a shot was fired, the English apparently regarding them with superstitious awe. Upon Joan's return to the city the people thronged about her, sweeping her with them to her lodgings, where they nearly broke down the entrance to Jacques Boucher's home.

That evening she again spoke to the English, this time from the city walls. They replied as cruelly as before but though she was within range they made no attempt to reach her with their cannons. Perhaps no gunner could be brought to aim at the "witch." The appearance in the sunset of that fearless figure in white armor, uttering such warnings as even the commonest soldier could understand, had an effect hard to realize today. Next morning she even rode out on the fields in the direction of the English forts, followed by a great crowd of the people of Orléans. They were sure that no harm could befall them, and certain it is they all came back safely. Joan and her company were within easy cannon range, probably within bowshot of the enemy, the five bastilles being no more than a third of a mile from the city walls which they had often bombarded.

A word about the situation of Orléans. These five bastilles, or stone towers, some of them with outer embankments called *boulevards*, were located to the west of Orléans in the general direction of Blois. A few hundred yards apart, they were in-

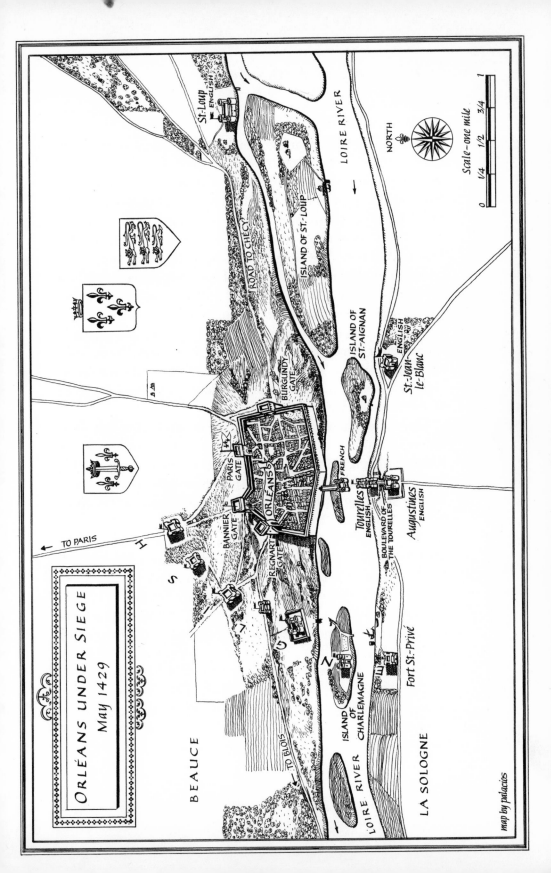

ORLÉANS UNDER SIEGE
May 1429

BEAUCE

TO PARIS →

TO BLOIS →

LOIRE RIVER

LA SOLOGNE

map by palacios

Scale – one mile

NORTH

0   1/4   1/2   3/4   1

LOIRE RIVER

ISLAND OF ST.-LOUP

ST.-LOUP
ENGLISH

ROAD TO CHECY

ISLAND OF ST.-AIGNAN

ST.-JEAN
le-Blanc
ENGLISH

BURGUNDY
GATE

PARIS
GATE

ORLÉANS

BANNIER
GATE

REGNART GATE

FRENCH

Tourelles
ENGLISH

BOULEVARD OF
THE TOURELLES

Augustines
ENGLISH

ISLAND
OF
CHARLEMAGNE

Fort St.-Privé

tended by the English to control the entrance to Orléans in that direction. It was between these fortresses that Joan had intended to march her army straight into Orléans. To the eastward of the city was the fortified church of St.-Loup, supposed to control the river in that direction though as we have seen Joan and her provision train had entered from that side. On an island below Orléans was a fortress and across from it on the south bank, another, so that the river was really well guarded in that direction. The English also held the south end of the bridge, and the near-by fortress of the Augustines, with still another fortress a distance up the river, that of St.-Jean-le-Blanc, which Joan had wished to attack on the evening of her arrival. The reader cannot be expected to keep these various points in his head, for which reason a map, drawn as simply as possible, has been provided. The sandy bed of the Loire is always changing. The islands as shown bear no close resemblance to those of the present day.

There is one more incident of the few days when Joan was waiting for the return of her army that is worth remembering. Riding through the streets, encouraging the people and the soldiers, she happened upon a rich merchant who unluckily was fiercely swearing at the moment when Joan appeared. The Maid briskly dismounted and laid her hand on his throat.

"Ah, friend," she said, "dare you forswear our Lord and Master? In God's name, you will recant before I leave here!"

The rich man was startled and ashamed.

"I am sorry, Joan," he said, "I will make amends."

Joan was no meek and lowly reformer. She believed in sudden and vigorous measures. One is reminded of Christ and the moneychangers.

X

THE MAID OF ORLEANS

Joan rides to battle

It was on the morning of the fourth of May, 1429, that Joan of Arc at the head of five hundred men rode out of Orléans to meet and escort into that city Dunois and D'Aulon, who were bringing back the army from Blois. How far she went on the road to meet them we do not know, but when she had greeted Dunois and her captains and troops, all marched into Orléans without the slightest interference from the English forts. Father Pasquerel, who was among them, in charge of the priests and the holy banner, thus described the entrance: "Having known of our coming Joan came out to meet us and all together we entered the city. There was no resistance; we introduced the supplies under the very eyes of the English. This was a marvelous thing. The English were in great strength and multitude, excellently armed and ready for battle, and they saw that the King's men made a sorry figure by comparison. They saw us, they heard the chanting of our priests, in the midst of which I was, carrying the banner. Very well, they made no movement, and neither priests nor soldiers were attacked."

Joan's army was reduced in size, some of it having melted away as she had feared it might. The English were in great need of provisions, yet they did not attack. They were as if under a spell, unable to move or make a sound. And thus, as she had planned in the beginning, the Maid in white armor and carrying her banner led her army safely past the forts where were Talbot and the English. The people held this to be the work of God, and became eager to attack.

Joan, herself, was in high spirits. While she was happily eating her midday meal with Jean d'Aulon, Dunois came in with a report that English troops from the north, commanded by Sir John Fastolf, were marching with supplies for the enemy. A hearty girl of seventeen, the Maid could not repress her spirits. With excitement and good humor, she answered Dunois: "On my faith, I command thee that as soon as thou shalt know of the coming of this Fastolf thou shalt let me know; for if he pass without my knowing I will have thy head taken off!"

Dunois as good-humoredly replied: "Thou needst have no doubt, Joan, but that I will let thee know."

There was no plan to give battle that day nor on the next, which was Ascension Day. The tired army and its leaders needed a rest. The soldiers of Orléans, now full of confidence, could not wait and made up an attacking party. At the home of Jacques Boucher the weary D'Aulon had lain down on a couch, and not far away Madame Boucher and Joan had also composed themselves for a nap. All at once the Maid sprang up in great excitement.

"What is the matter? What has happened?" called D'Aulon and Madame Boucher together.

"In God's name," cried Joan, "my Voice has told me to go

against the English, but I do not know if I must go at their
bastilles or against Fastolf, who would bring them supplies!"

D'Aulon and Madame Boucher hastily collected the Maid's
arms. Meantime a great noise arose in the street and a cry that
the enemy was destroying the French. Joan went plunging down
the stairs to arouse her page, De Contes.

"Ha, graceless boy!" she cried, "you did not tell me that the
blood of France was flowing! Go quickly for my horse!"

She ran back up the stairs, where D'Aulon and Madame
Boucher quickly armed her. As she reached the street De Contes
appeared with the horse.

"My standard!" she cried. "My standard!"

De Contes flew up the stairs and passed the banner to her
through an upper window. Standard in hand she left at a gallop
in the direction of the tumult. Joan of Arc was riding to battle!
Fire flew from under her horse's feet!

"Ride after her!" shouted Madame Boucher to De Contes,
which the page did. What glory for a boy of fifteen!

D'Aulon, meantime, had armed himself and a minute later
came pounding after them, overtaking them at the Burgundy
gate, beyond which was the fighting. The French had attacked
the fortified church of St.-Loup and as usual were getting the
worst of it. As Joan, D'Aulon and De Contes reached the city
gate a wounded man was being carried in. The Maid checked
her horse.

"Who is that you are carrying?" she asked.

"A wounded Frenchman."

"French blood! I never see it that my hair does not rise!"

They swept through into the field. French reinforcements
were now pouring from the city. Joan waved her standard.

"Forward with God!" and they charged in the direction of
St.-Loup. The English, catching sight of a white standard and
a figure in shining armor bearing down upon them, became
panic-stricken. A moment later they were stampeding back to

their fort, the French in close pursuit. Then soon it was all over; the terrified enemy, unable to resist, was cut down or captured. St.-Loup had been a church and some of the English, hastily putting on robes they found there, claimed mercy as priests. Joan ordered these to be spared, unwilling to violate even the appearance of piety. Also, to the sound of a trumpet, she commanded that there should be no pillage of the already desecrated church.

The battle was over, the fighting for the day at an end. St.-Loup had fallen. One hundred and forty of the English had been killed and forty taken prisoners; apparently none had escaped. The battles of that day were seldom on a grand scale but they were bloody.

Surrounded by her army, Joan, victorious but sorrowful, rode back to her lodgings. It was her first battle, her first bloodshed. The little girl who had "known neither how to ride nor conduct war," who in tears and trembling heard the command as to what she must do, had led soldiers to battle and seen men struck down to die. Now again she wept at this piteous need. Of the fallen English she said: "Those poor people—they died without confession! I would I might have saved them!"

She confessed herself to Father Pasquerel and commanded him to warn her soldiers to confess and give thanks for victory. "For," she said, "otherwise I will no longer aid them or remain in their company." Further, she told him: "In five days the siege of Orléans will be raised, and there will not remain an Englishman before the city." And added: "On tomorrow, the day of the Ascension of our Lord, I will not arm myself, neither will any soldier go out of the city to battle without previous confession." Night came down to the ringing of bells and shouts of rejoicing in the streets of Orléans, sounds that fell ominously on English ears. Joan of Arc, a peasant girl of seventeen, had given her soldiers victory, their first in a weary time.

Capture of the Augustines

Joan next morning sent her final summons and warning to the English; it ran:

You men of England who have no right in the kingdom of France, the King of Heaven sends word to you and commands, by me, Joan the Maid, that you quit your bastilles and return to your own country. Otherwise I will cause you such confusion that it will be of perpetual memory. This is what I write to you for the third and last time and I will not write to you any more. *Jesus Mary.*

Joan the Maid.

I would have sent my letter more honestly but you retain my heralds; you have retained my herald Guienne. Return him to me and I will send you some of your men taken at the Battle of St.-Loup; for they were not all dead.

Taking a thread, Joan tied her letter to the end of an arrow and ordered an archer to shoot it among the English, crying: "Read, here is news!"

The arrow reached the English, who read the letter and began shouting with great clamor: "News from the Jezebel of the Armagnacs!" and other evil words, at which Joan sobbed and wept, asking God to help her; but presently became calm, comforted by her Voices.

A council of war was held at which it was agreed that the next attack should be made across the river, to get possession of the Tourelles which controlled the end of the bridge on that side of the Loire.

The following morning—it was Friday May 6—this attack was begun. Pasquerel rose at break of day, confessed Joan and chanted mass before all the people. A great number of boats had been assembled under the walls of Orléans and these now ferried the army to the island of St.-Aignan above the bridge. This island lay very close to the south bank; the narrow channel between could be spanned by two boats on which the soldiers could march over. The fort of St.-Jean-le-Blanc was just there; their first purpose was to attack it. Joan and La Hire did not cross immediately. The troops, hot for battle, did not wait for them but rushed on St.-Jean-le-Blanc only to find it abandoned, the enemy having taken refuge in the larger and stronger bastille of the Augustines near the end of the bridge. The eager French pushed toward this fort but the enemy, seeing that the Maid was not with them, regained confidence and with their "terrible hurrah" sallied forth in a charge so fierce and sudden that the old-time fear again fell upon the French and sent them scurrying in the direction of their boats. It was just at this time that Joan and La Hire, each with a horse in a boat, landed from another part of the island, and seeing at a glance what had happened, quickly mounted.

"In God's name, forward boldly!" Joan shouted, and with La Hire rode straight at the enemy.

Instantly all was changed. English and French, seeing the white armor and the banner, were equally inspired—the one with fear, the other with courage. The French literally raced with each other to reach the enemy, now stampeding to their stronghold. Arriving just behind the English, the French found a powerful and brave English soldier, a veritable giant fully armed, blocking the entrance, standing in the narrow gateway, disdaining to close it. No more than one or two could get near him, not enough to make an impression on the huge combatant. D'Aulon turned to "Master John, the cannonier," whose weapon must have been one of the small hand pieces then recently invented, and bade him fire on this giant, which Master John did and with such good aim that with one shot he brought the great warrior to the ground.

Two knights who had joined hands and raced each other to the fort now rushed in, all the others following, attacking groups of the enemy, who made no very stout resistance. It was St.-Loup over again except that some of the English escaped to the bastille of the Tourelles, the towers at the end of the bridge. No assistance came from the Tourelles nor from any English stronghold on either side of the river. The English were not leaving their strongholds to face that hair-lifting figure in white armor that in the sunset had warned them from the city walls. That night, indeed, those in St.-Privé, lower down, burned their own defenses and escaped to the bastilles across the river, leaving to their fate their comrades in the Tourelles who being hemmed in had no choice but to remain. The Tourelles, however, were very strong; few believed they could be taken.

The French army camped that night in the Augustines. The Maid herself was persuaded to return to her lodgings at Orléans for proper rest and food, in preparation for the heavy work ahead. Father Pasquerel testified that though it was Friday, she did not fast that night, having so much to do. He added this interesting and curious incident: "She was finishing her repast, when there came to her a noble and valiant captain whose name I do not recall. He said to Joan: 'The captains are assembled in council. They recognize that there are not many French as compared with the English and that it has been by the grace of God that they have obtained some advantage. The city now being full of provision we can hold it easily while waiting succor from the King. Wherefore, the Council does not find it expedient that the soldiers tomorrow make an attack.'

"Joan answered: 'You have been at your Council and I have been at mine. Now be assured that the Council of the Lord will fulfill itself and prevail and that yours will fail.' And addressing herself to me, who was near her, said: 'Rise tomorrow very early, earlier than even today, and do the best you are able. It will be necessary to keep always near me, for tomorrow I shall have much to do and greater need of you than I have ever had. Tomorrow the blood will flow from my body, above the breast.' "

Joan had foretold her wound, both in Chinon, to the King,

and to persons in Tours. In the letter already mentioned, written two weeks before the event, the writer, a Flemish diplomat, tells of the Maid and of her statement that she is to be wounded at Orléans by a shaft but will not die of it; also that before the end of summer the King will be crowned at Reims. This letter is still preserved in the library of Brussels.

The Tourelles

In spite of her two splendid successes Joan was still opposed by some of her captains. Possibly they were jealous of her, or perhaps the Tourelles, rising dark and grim in the night, overawed them. There is a story that next morning Raoul de Gaucourt, military governor of Orléans, tried to prevent Joan leaving the city and was denounced by her in rather severe terms. Some sort of opposition there must have been to the attack on the Tourelles but it proved of no avail. Father Pasquerel rose an hour after midnight and celebrated mass. As Joan was making ready to leave her lodgings a man came bringing a fish for her breakfast, an *alose* (in English, a shad). Seeing it she said to Madame Boucher: "Keep it until evening, because this evening I will bring you a *godon* [French term for the English] and will return by the way of the bridge."

With Pasquerel and a troop of soldiers, Joan now crossed the river and went to the assault of the bastille of the Tourelles, the stout fortress commanded by Glasdale, who had reviled her.

The defenses of the bridge were very simple: at the entrance, a short distance from the Augustines, there was a steep embankment or *boulevard*, in front of which was a *fosse*, a deep, dry ditch. Behind the embankment was a wooden drawbridge connecting it with the Tourelles, two great stone towers which stood on the end of the bridge itself. Beyond these there was a gap in the bridge of several feet, broken out by the English to prevent attack from the Orléans side. It seemed a complete defense and may well have discouraged Joan's captains. The

Duke of Alençon later testified that with a small force in the Tourelles he could have defied an entire army.

Joan of Arc did not even know the word discouragement. Arriving on the scene, she summoned her captains, unfurled her banner and ordered a general attack on the outer embankment. At once ladders began to rise and shouting men to scale them; arrows began to fly, the small cannon of that day to roar and fling their wicked little balls of chipped stone. And at the top of the embankment were the desperate English with axes, lances, *guisarmes* (a long steel weapon, hooked and sharpened at the end), leaden maces—the owners of these fierce weapons thrusting, smiting, stabbing, even with their bare hands flinging the ladders back, their bowmen sending flight after flight of arrows into the throng of attacking men.

A stirring picture of medieval warfare it was; and amid it all a figure in white armor, encouraging her soldiers, lending a hand to the work—her standard, held aloft by a bearer, floating before her on the wind.

De Contes, that brave boy, was there and told how she called to them continually: "Have good heart! Do not fall back, you will have the bastille soon!"

Through the May morning and deep into the afternoon the strife continued. Then came what seemed disaster: that which the Maid had foretold occurred. She was setting up a ladder when a bolt from a crossbow fired directly from above, struck her between the shoulder and the throat with such force that it pierced armor and body through, the length of half a foot.

She was helped from the field, the cruel shaft was withdrawn and the upper part of her armor removed. Oh, the fierce tearing pain, the jetting blood! Soldiers wished to "charm" the wound but this she refused, believing such work to be a sin. She willingly accepted a dressing of olive oil and lard, weeping and lamenting meanwhile, just a girl of seventeen, sorely wounded. But then her Voices came, that of Saint Catherine, as she said later, and the pain eased. Confessing briefly, with her page's help she donned her armor and returned to the field.

By this time the face of the battle had changed. The Maid's misfortune had given new confidence to the English. They had drawn blood from the witch in white armor; she had crawled off to die. Correspondingly the French had lost courage; without the Maid they would be where they had been before her coming. They were worn out; the hour was near sunset; as Joan appeared on the field a retreat was being sounded. Hurrying to Dunois, she called out:

"Not yet! not yet! I beg that you wait a little!"

Assisted to mount her horse, she rode to a near-by vineyard to pray. A few moments later she returned, seized her standard, planted it on the brink of the *fosse* and ordered a charge. Seeing her again among them the soldiers, with renewed courage, ran to the ladders.[1]

And now the enemy looking down became terrified. Only a little while ago the witch had been carried from the field to die. She had returned and after working some deadly spell in the vineyard, was about to destroy them. "They shuddered," according to Dunois, "and were filled with terror." Joan called out to the English commander: "Glasdale, Glasdale, surrender to the King of Heaven! You called me Jezebel, but I have great pity for your soul and for your followers!"

The English had still another reason for their terror. The people of Orléans had been busy and had timed their assistance well. In the midst of the final assault a fire raft loaded with a quantity of inflammable material had been ignited and from the end of the isle of St.-Aignan carefully drifted exactly under the wooden drawbridge which connected the outer embankment with the Tourelles. Busy with the attack, the English had not noticed this maneuver. Their first warning of it was a cloud of rising smoke, the smell of pitch, the fierce crackle of flames. For them no further interest in the French assault, but only a

1. This is Dunois's account. De Contes testified that she said, as it seemed to him: "When you see the wind carry the banner to the wall, it will be yours"— a version which imaginative writers have turned into an incident still more dramatic.

general dash for safety. A good portion of them must have crossed but then the burning structure gave way and all on it, including Glasdale and other nobles, true knights last to go, were plunged into the swollen river and being armored, gave no further sign.

Those who had managed to cross to the Tourelles found themselves little better off. The Orléans carpenters had prepared a narrow bridge made from a long trough, or gutter, which they now pushed across the broken-out gap behind the Tourelles. Over it passed a knight of the Order of Rhodes, fully armed, and behind him many others. To the enemy looking down into the flame-lit smoke and night the narrow support was invisible —the Orléans soldiers seemed to be coming through the air. With fire behind and below, completely hemmed in, the English made no further resistance. Not one escaped; all not killed or drowned were captured.

Though he had called her evil names, Joan lamented the death of Glasdale. Sorrowful, weary, sorely wounded and tri-umphant—to the sound of bells and the chanting of the people of Orléans—the Maid rode back by the bridge as she had prom-ised, bringing her *godon*, many *godons*, to supper. She did not eat the *alose* saved for her. At her lodging a surgeon dressed her wound, after which she took a few slices of bread dipped in water and reddened with wine, and so the eventful day ended. Did her wound throb and burn and break her sleep? Or did Saint Catherine again soothe away the pain? We have her own statement that it was cured in a fortnight and that meantime she did not cease to ride.

Joan completes her sign

Early next morning—it was Sunday the eighth of May, 1429—the report was brought to Joan that the English facing Orléans had left their bastilles and arrayed themselves in order of battle. The Maid rose and because of her wound armored herself only in a light coat of mail. As she left the house she was asked: "Is it wrong to fight on Sunday?"

She answered: "We must hold mass."

Her army had formed outside the walls, facing the enemy. A portable altar was brought and two masses celebrated, which the Maid and her soldiers heard with great devotion. The service ended, Joan, still kneeling, asked: "Do the English face our way?"

She was told that they had turned toward the château of Meung.

"In God's name," she said, "they are going. Let them go while we give thanks to God and pursue them no farther, since today is Sunday."

Less than two months before, at Poitiers, Joan had said: "I did not come to Poitiers to work signs. Take me to Orléans and I will show you the sign for which I was sent."

She had kept her word; she had shown her sign. A situation which had baffled the French captains, kept a city in terror and a king in walled retirement for nearly seven months, a girl of seventeen had relieved in three days.

The English had decamped, leaving much material; also, their sick and certain prisoners—among them, by one account, Joan's herald Guienne. The people of Orléans at once ordered the bastilles pulled down.

And on that same Sunday the city joined in great procession, in which churchmen, soldiers and citizens mingled. It was the first of the *fêtes* to be held in honor of the Maid of Orléans, for such she had become to them, so to remain until this day.

XI

THE CAMPAIGN OF THE LOIRE

"Come to Reims and receive your crown!"

Her work in Orléans complete, Joan's plan now was to seek out the King and urge him to come to Reims and receive his crown. Disregarding the soreness of her wound she went off the next morning after taking leave of the people of Orléans, who gathered about her weeping for joy, offering as gifts whatever she might desire. She asked nothing but their good will and with Dunois and her military household set out for Chinon by the south bank of the Loire, pausing to give thanks at the famous shrine of Cléry, where her name, with that of Dunois, is still recorded.

As Joan rode through the golden May weather to carry her tidings to the King other riders from Orléans were speeding in every direction, bearing to every corner of Europe news of her great victory. Foreign news writers, forerunners of today's journalists, were sending it to kings, princes, churchmen in every

capital. The peasant girl of Domrémy had been found to be all that she had claimed. She had become the most important figure in France. The great churchman, Jean Gerson, then in Lyons, issued a statement in which he called her a worthy sister of Deborah and Judith, comparing her with Saint Catherine. The Archbishop of Embrun declared that the Maid was to be obeyed as a messenger of God and spoke of her as "an angel of the armies of the Lord." The Duke of Bedford—uncle of the little English King and ruling in his stead as "Regent of England and France" —fearing an uprising in Paris, hurried to the castle of Vincennes and sent out a general summons for soldiers to combat the powers of this "disciple and limb of Satan." Few would respond, for the news of what had happened at Orléans was reaching Burgundian and English soldiers as well as their leaders. Joan as she rode knew that this would be so and that if the King with her army would set out at once for Reims, few would oppose his progress.

She had expected to go to Chinon to meet Charles, but the news of her victory had outrun her and he was on his way to Tours. She arrived there a little before him and with her banner in her hand rode forward to greet him. An old chronicle says: "Then the young girl bowed low before the King, who bade her sit upright, and it is thought that he gladly would have kissed her for the joy that he felt." In all history there are not many such moments: a peasant girl of seventeen offering to a king his kingdom.

And now side by side they entered Tours, while the shouting, weeping populace thronged about them and the bells rang and many knelt or pressed forward, to kiss or touch the Maid's hands, her feet, her clothing, even her horse and were in danger of being trodden down. One may be certain that among that swaying mass was little Héliote Poulvoir and that later Joan sought out the painter's pretty daughter, who rejoiced and wept to welcome back from battle this miracle-working comrade who had delivered a city and had been wounded, who was a great heroine—almost a saint.

"Come to Reims," Joan urged the King, "come to Reims and receive your crown!" but the timid Charles and his time-serving counselors hesitated. Cities in English hands were along the way. In spite of the "sign" she had shown, Charles and his court did not entirely share her faith. Her wound, they said, must have time to heal. Dunois, meantime, would attack Jargeau, twelve miles east of Orléans and still in English hands.

Joan, against her will, was taken to Loches, where the King had a fine château which he could now enjoy without fear of his enemies. At Loches, Joan was surrounded by luxury and idolized by the people but she fretted and grieved, for she saw her army, unpaid and poorly fed, melting away; and she counted the passing of her precious days.

At last one day she knocked at the door of the King's apartment where he sat with two of his counselors; a moment later she entered and, falling on her knees to Charles, said: "Noble Dauphin, hold no longer so many of these interminable councils, but come at once to Reims and receive your rightful crown."

"Is it your Council that tells you this?" asked one of those present.

"Yes," she replied, "and I am much stimulated thereby."

"Would you not explain, here in the presence of the King, the manner of your Council when it speaks to you?"

Joan answered: "I think I understand what you want to know and I will tell it to you willingly."

"Joan," said the King, "is it truly your wish, before the persons here present, to declare what is asked of you?"

"Yes," she answered, and added: "When I am baffled in some manner because someone does not wish to credit the thing I speak on the part of God, I retire apart and pray to God, complaining that those to whom I speak are hard of belief. My prayer to God finished, I hear a Voice that says to me: 'Daughter of God, go, go, go! I will aid thee, go!' And when I hear this Voice I have great joy. I would like always to hear it."

Dunois, who was present and told of this, added that as she spoke she seemed transported. This brave soldier had returned to Loches to get the King's sanction for raising a new army under Joan's leadership. His attack on Jargeau had failed. Without the Maid, the French still could not win. Dunois said that hearing these words from Joan the King became very joyous and decided to believe her. He would go to Reims but they would first take some places along the Loire.

"And I saw her mount her horse— all in white"

Joan had been about ten days at Loches and her wound was as good as healed. With Alençon, her *beau duc*, who was to be military head of the new expedition, she at once began to collect men and supplies. Captains who had fought at Orléans and who had faith in the Maid came with their troops to Romorantin, where they were ordered to assemble. Charles meantime conferred armorial bearings on Joan, perhaps thinking this would give her more prestige in raising troops: as if any decoration could add to her prestige in the eyes of those who had been with her at Orléans. "They came," says one old chronicler, "more to accompany Joan the Maid than for any other reason."

Money was harder to raise than men but here also the Maid's name proved a magic word. Cities gave supplies and support came from private sources—from nobles little able to afford it after the heavy ransoms which most of them had paid following the disaster of Verneuil. A young noble, Guy de Laval, scion of one of the oldest families in France, on the way with his brother to join the new army, wrote a letter to his people which shows the spirit of the moment. The writer tells of the scarcity of funds and urges his mother not to spare his estates either by sale or mortgage, to the end that money may be raised in support of the cause. The writer had seen Joan and his letter is especially fortunate in the lovely picture it presents of her. It was written from Selles, where the Maid gave warm welcome to the brothers De Laval, "she being fully armed except the head."

And there seemed something wholly divine in her manner and to see her and to hear her . . . and I saw her mount her horse—armed all in white all except her head, a little ax in her hand—on a black courser, that at the entrance of her lodging plunged fiercely and would not suffer her to mount; whereupon she said: "Lead him to the cross," which was before the near-by church on the road. And then she mounted without him moving any more than if he had been bound. Then she turned toward the church which was close by and said in a very womanly voice: "You, priests and men of the church, form procession and make prayers to God." After which she set out on her way, saying: "Forward! Forward!" her standard furled, carried by a graceful page, her little ax in her hand.

To how many Joan's face and manner gave the impression of having in them "something divine!" Unhappily, no one left any worthy description of her; we have little more than the words of D'Aulon that she was "*belle et bien formée*" (beautiful and well formed).

The new army collected at Romorantin, Joan saw it safely on its march for the Loire with Alençon overtaking it at Orléans. It was a very good army numbering five or six thousand men, well equipped for siege work. Jargeau was twelve miles up the river and the march upon it was not delayed. The English commanders of the town were the Duke of Suffolk and his two brothers, John and Alexander de la Pole. They had no great force but their defenses were very strong, by many believed impregnable.

Upon the army's arrival before Jargeau there was the usual discussion among the captains. Some were for the assault, others against it. Joan bade them be without fear. "Do not hesitate to assault the English," she said. "God conducts our work. If I had not this assurance I would rather guard sheep than expose myself to so great perils."

The men pressed forward, thinking to capture the outskirts of the town. As they did so the English made a sudden sortie and drove the French back. Seeing this, Joan seized her standard.

"Have good heart," she called to them. "Forward with God!"

A little later the English had retreated to their defenses and the French camped that night in the adjoining suburbs. In the darkness, approaching the great walls of the citadel, the Maid called to those within: "Surrender to the King of Heaven and to the noble King Charles and go away. Otherwise He will destroy you!"

She thought it right to warn those she was about to attack. Also, she well knew the effect this would have on the men, even upon the officers. No answer came from the fort; perhaps Suffolk had heard of the fate of Glasdale after calling the Maid an evil name.

No guard was set that night by the French, who seemed to have full faith in Joan's protection. They were not attacked and early next morning the heavy guns were brought forward for the assault. There was a difference of opinion among the leaders, some being in favor of delay. Joan's policy was to strike swiftly; her heralds began summoning the soldiers, crying: "To the assault!" Joan herself called to Alençon, "Forward, noble duke, to the assault!" And as he hesitated she added: "Doubt not, the hour is good when God pleases. One must work when God wills. Work, and God will work also."

Alençon himself told of this and how a little later she said to him: "Ah, noble duke, hast thou fear? Knowest thou not I have promised thy wife to bring thee back safe and sound?"

"In fact," said Alençon, "when I left my wife to come to the army with Joan, my wife said to her: 'Joan, I am much afraid for my husband. He is no more than out of prison and has been obliged to spend so much money for ransom that I would gladly see him remain at home.' To which Joan answered: 'Madame, be without fear; I will bring him back safe to you and in better health than he is now.' "

Alençon had always full faith in Joan and it was here quickly justified. The English guns on the ramparts opened fire and stone cannon balls began to work damage to the French. Joan said to him: "Step aside from there; if you do not that gun will kill you." The duke obeyed and a moment later a ball from the gun killed a man who had taken his place.

Joan now urged forward the assault on the English defenses. As the soldiers rushed to the walls, the Duke of Suffolk called out that he wished to speak to Alençon. In the tumult the latter failed to hear this and the assault proceeded. Joan started up a ladder, standard in hand. A stone from above struck her helmet, felling her to the earth. An instant later she was on her feet, calling to her soldiers: "Friends, friends, up! up! Our Lord has condemned the English. At this moment they are ours! Have good heart!"

It was the Tourelles over again. Friend and foe had seen her struck down, only to spring up anew and lead the charge. The French rushed at the walls; the English made a feeble resistance, then fled for the bridge across the Loire. A few escaped, the rest were killed and captured. Suffolk himself was made prisoner with one of his brothers; the other, Alexander de la Pole, was killed. There is a story that Suffolk declared he would surrender only to the Maid herself but this seems to be a fable. Joan and Alençon with their army and prisoners returned to Orléans. English power at Jargeau had been utterly destroyed.

The cloth for two fine garments

At Orléans the Maid was received with the usual celebration. To the people she seemed as marvelous as an angel from the skies. Captains and soldiers were grandly fêted; re-enforcement came pouring in.

Exalted by her victories, the Maid was not without moments of deep sorrow, for she loathed the shedding of blood. The shouting people, the waving banners, the festooned streets that everywhere greeted her, tribute to glorious conquest, had been paid for with the lives of brave men. At Orléans, however, there was waiting one reward that must have given her a special satisfaction. This was an order from the poet Duke Charles, prisoner in England, to his treasurer, Jacques Boucher, to pay thirteen écus of gold to a merchant and a tailor for the cloth and the making of two fine garments, one of crimson and the other of green, both to be richly lined and finished with white satin and other materials, all very costly as shown by the price—the same to be completed and delivered to Joan the Maid, "in consideration of the good and agreeable services that the said Maid has rendered us in the encounter with the English, ancient enemies of my lord the King and of ourselves."

The garments were named as "a robe and a *huque*," and we are not entirely clear today as to their form, but one of them was a kind of overdress slashed at the sides to be worn above her armor. Joan could hardly have been less than happy in this fine remembrance from the duke in exile and she was human enough and girl enough to love the gift for its own sake. She had a taste for the choice in dress and became passionately fond of beautiful armor. How different this new robe from the patched red gown she had worn to Vaucouleurs!

The Maid could not be persuaded to linger at Orléans. Alençon's squire, Perceval de Cagny, who kept a record of events and later wrote a memoir, says that on the evening of the sec-

ond day she called her *beau duc* and said to him: "I wish tomorrow, after dinner, to see those of Meung. Give orders that
the company be ready to leave at that hour."

Meung, twelve miles below Orléans, was another town in
English hands. The army marched according to orders by the
south bank, arriving in time to capture the bridgehead after a
skirmish. They camped there and leaving a detachment to hold
the bridge, next morning pushed on four miles farther to the
English stronghold of Beaugency where they expected stout
resistance. But at the first attack the English withdrew to the
great square tower of the château and that night offered to
abandon the town at daybreak with certain of their belongings.
The agreement was made and they gladly enough left at the
hour named.

Just here occurred an event, important at the moment and to
become far more so as time passed. Some years before, the King's
chief officer, Arthur of Richemont, Constable of France, had
been the means of connecting Georges de La Trémouille with
Charles's court. The plotting La Trémouille had lost no time in
undermining his patron and sponsor. Always at Charles's ear,
he invented such reports as presently caused the weak, persuad-
able King to estrange Richemont and deny him the court. So
bitter toward Richemont did Charles become that his powerful
military aid was rejected, his friendship with any member of
the court forbidden. The Constable, however, on his own account had continued the fight for France. Now, suddenly, on
this June morning at Beaugency, he appeared with his lords at
the head of a thousand picked men, to petition Joan to make
his peace with the King.

The situation was a difficult one. All well knew the King's
orders. When Richemont's approach was reported Alençon
went so far as to declare that if the Constable came he would
go. The Maid seems to have said very little. A great decisive
battle with the English was likely to occur at any hour. Fastolf's
force, so long reported, was not far away and had been joined

by troops under Talbot, a part of those driven from Orléans. This army Joan meant to destroy. Richemont was a distinguished leader, his aid most important. Her business was to secure it— to reconcile the French captains. A fortunate circumstance furnished an opportunity.

The Constable with his lords having arrived on the scene, Joan drew him a little away from the others to discuss the matter. It is said that Richemont knelt to the Maid, which in courtesy he may well have done. They were talking quietly when one of La Hire's men reported to Alençon that a body of English were approaching: "The enemy is marching on us," he said. "We are going to have him facing us."

Joan, within earshot, was not so deeply engaged that she did not catch the drift of the messenger's report. Calling to Alençon, she asked: "What did that soldier say?"

The message was made known to her. Whereupon, addressing herself to Richemont, she said: "Ah, fair Constable, you did not come because of me, but since you are come, you are welcome."

Such was the beginning of what was to prove of great moment in the history of France. It would take time, for La Trémouille would long and bitterly oppose it. But a day of full reconciliation would arrive, and its beginning was that morning at Beaugency in the face of a threatening army.

"Have good spurs, all of you"

Talbot, with a small body of men, had met Fastolf at Janville, a village to the north of Orléans, and urged him at once to march to Meung, where his own main army was quartered, the French holding the captured bridgehead across the river. Talbot and Fastolf united would then give battle to the Maid's forces.

Fastolf did not like the idea. He said that with the French

exalted by their recent victories and the English in a like manner frightened and discouraged, such a battle might well prove
a disaster. His idea was to let the Loire troops make the best
terms they could while he and Talbot waited further reinforce-
ment from Bedford in Paris. Talbot, smarting from his defeat at
Orléans, vowed that with the aid of God and Saint George
and such men as would follow him he would push on and fight.
A month earlier he had withdrawn his army from the bastilles
before Orléans, showing no fight whatever; what had caused
this sudden change of heart? That Talbot was held as a wise
and valiant soldier is certain and Fastolf finally yielded. The
captains were ordered to be ready next morning to march on
Meung and Beaugency. They departed in the dawn, pennons
flying, making a brave sight, though sick at heart, riding to
meet the "witch of Orléans and Jargeau" and therefore to their
deaths, as most of them believed. When they had gone a little
way Fastolf again protested, declaring that they were but a
handful and in no wise fit to stand against the Maid's army. One
cannot help comparing such admonition with Joan's fearless:
"Forward boldly! Have good heart, they are ours!" whether
her troops were few or many and when for years they had
known nothing but defeat.

Surely no army ever went forward with so little heart as
Fastolf's. Yet, Talbot insisting, they moved on in perfect order
taking the straight road for the Loire. This was the force reported by La Hire's soldier to Alençon at the moment when the
Maid spoke with Richemont at Beaugency.

In spite of their victories the French captains were not without doubts. Alençon, military commander of the expedition,
said to Joan: "What shall I do?"

The Maid answered, loudly enough for all to hear, "Have
good spurs, all of you."

At this some of the captains asked: "What did you say? Are
we, then, to turn our backs?"

"No, the English will turn *their* backs. They will not defend themselves and will be beaten. You will need good spurs to follow them." Again she said: "Strike boldly, they will take to flight." She added that it would not take long.

The captains disposed themselves in order of battle and after waiting a considerable time for the English moved forward to meet them, taking a position on a low hilltop about a mile from Beaugency. The English, believing that they were at once to be attacked, dismounted and planted their spears—butts in the ground, points forward—a tactic which had won for them earlier in the year at Rouvray. They now sent forward two heralds proposing that three knights be chosen from each side to try the justice of their cause. This did not suit Joan. To her mind the only thing to do with this English army was to destroy it. She said: "Go to your camp for today, for it is late enough; but tomorrow, at the pleasure of God and Our Lady, we shall see you nearer."

The English did not keep their position. During the night they withdrew to Meung, where they bombarded the French garrison across the river. By morning even Talbot was no longer recklessly brave. The French force of the day before had looked very large to him. Joan's words had sounded ominous; they reminded him of her warnings at Orléans. Moreover, with morning came news of the English surrender at Beaugency, unknown to him the day before. He agreed with Fastolf to retreat. Gathering up the force that had been holding Meung, the combined armies set out across the level land called the Beauce toward Paris. Knowing the French would be quickly after them they took the field hastily but as they retreated northward disposed themselves in good marching order, their retreat led by an English knight bearing a white standard. Joan's banner of victory was white; the English may have thought there was some special virtue in that color.

The English power broken at Patay

We left the French army in battle order on a low hill but they seem to have camped at Beaugency. During the night they must have heard the bombardment of the bridgehead at Meung, four miles distant, but it was eight next morning before they were in marching order, which would bring them to Meung about nine. The guns had long since ceased there and the enemy had vanished. Gathering up her detachment left to hold the bridgehead, the Maid prepared to follow them.

But now again there was doubt and hesitation. Some of the captains had no taste for the combined forces of Fastolf and Talbot. The Maid's intent was clear enough; according to Alençon she said:

"In God's name we must fight them! If they were hung to the clouds we would have them! The noble King will have today the greatest victory he has known in a long time. My Council has told me they are all ours."

"Where shall we find them?" she was asked. To which she answered: "Ride with confidence; we shall have good guidance."

The level Beauce, now a plain of wheat, was in that day covered with a bushy growth that could easily conceal an army. The French captains may have feared ambush but they now rode forward, an advance guard of sixty or eighty picked warriors mounted on "flowers of horses" riding ahead to make discovery. Joan had wished to lead this guard but was persuaded to leave it to La Hire on the grounds that her presence would be of more value to the main army.

It is eighteen miles from Meung to the village of Patay and across this wide level, under a June sky, concealed from each other though but a little way apart, the two armies moved, pursuer and pursued. To report any approach of the French the English had scouts in the rear; and early in the afternoon when their army was about three miles from Patay, these brought in word that the Maid's army was coming, riding swiftly and in great strength.

Realizing that with their provision train and foot soldiers they could not escape, Talbot and Fastolf hastily prepared for battle. Orders were given to place the wagons along the hedges near Patay behind a forefront of spears planted in the favorite English fashion, butts in the ground; Talbot, meantime, with five hundred picked archers, would range himself along an open way by which the French were expected to come, thus hoping to hold them in check until the main defense could be formed. It was a good plan but the unexpected happened.

Joan had told her captains that they would have "good guidance." Probably she had no idea what it would be but she never made a truer prophecy. The French advance guard, La Hire at its head, had not yet sighted the English when suddenly in front of them a stag sprang up from among the bushes and bounded straight into the very midst of the English army. The soldiers, taken by surprise, eager to catch it and forgetful of the French, raised a great cry. La Hire and his eighty picked men dashed forward, sending back word to the main army that the enemy was found. Fastolf's defenses along the hedges were not yet formed. Talbot's archers were not yet in position. Seeing the French approach, the English army became a wild scramble of preparation.

At this point everything fell into confusion. The French, now fully aware of the English, came thundering forward. The picked eighty under La Hire, the Constable, De Boussac and Poton Saintrailles, that terrible quartette, struck Talbot's lane of archers and cut straight through them before they could fix their arrows. The English already forming at the hedges, seeing Fastolf hurrying with others to join them, thought him in full retreat, the battle already lost; at this the captain of the English advance guard, he of the white standard, without another look behind abandoned the hedges and with his men joined in a wild stampede of flight.

Nobody was more to blame than Fastolf. A day or two before he had frightened his men half to death and this was the result. The soldiers—those who could not escape—overwhelmed by fear and the suddenness of it all made a poor defense. La Hire and his eighty rode among them like demons. Talbot's archers were annihilated, Talbot himself was made prisoner. The main army under Joan and Alençon came up and completed the work. An old Burgundian chronicler, who was present, wrote of the scene: "They could at their will kill or capture as seemed good to them. The English were discomfited with small loss to the French. So there died of the said English fully two thousand men and there were taken two hundred prisoners."

Besides Talbot a number of English leaders were captured, including Lord Scales, son of the Earl of Warwick, whom we shall meet later. Fastolf was not captured but after watching the battle from a safe distance and, according to our old chronicler, "making the greatest dole ever man made," he joined the escaping remnant of his army and set out for Paris.

Little is known of Joan's active part in the Battle of Patay. That with her banner she was at the head of the main army is all we can be sure of, except for one incident told by her page Louis de Contes. A French soldier who conducted some English captives struck one of them on the head with such force that the man fell to the ground, dying. Joan, seeing this, quickly dismounted and hurrying to the fallen man had him confessed, meantime supporting his head on her arm, consoling him as much as was in her power. That is all we really know of Joan on the field of Patay, all we need to know. Exalted by victory, yet in the midst of it merciful and compassionate.

Talbot, a prisoner, was brought before Alençon—the Maid and Richemont being present. Alençon said to him: "You did not think this morning that this would happen to you."

Talbot replied: "It is the fortune of war." Joan and Talbot must have spoken together but there is no record of their words.

It was the afternoon of a long summer day that Patay was

fought, Saturday, June 18, 1429. Exactly a week earlier the Maid had attacked Jargeau, which had fallen next day. From Jargeau she had proceeded in the most workmanlike manner to envelop Meung and Beaugency and to strike Fastolf's impending army at Patay. Her plan had long included Fastolf. Six weeks earlier at Orléans she had playfully threatened to have Dunois's head if he let Fastolf pass without her knowledge. Now at last she had met Fastolf's army and destroyed it. Talbot's army was likewise scattered, Talbot himself a prisoner. Her prophecy that the King would have that day the greatest victory he had known "in a long time" had been more than fulfilled. Not in his lifetime had the King known such a victory. English power below Paris was broken forever.

XII

THE CORONATION JOURNEY

"Doubt not, you will gain all your kingdom"

By all military rules, Joan should now have
pushed on to Paris, a short two days' ride to the northward.
Her army was ample and full of courage. Paris would have
fallen, even opened its gates to her as so many cities did a month
later. Today, knowing all her story, we may well regret that
she did not lead her army straight to the capital; but if the
military leaders about her—Dunois, La Hire, the Constable, Alençon—mentioned Paris to her then, no hint of it remains. Certainly
her Voices did not or she would have gone. Time and again she
declared that she acted on their counsel. Her Voices had told
her to relieve Orléans, destroy the English and conduct the
King to his coronation at Reims. This she would obey to the
letter. Had the King been ready to start for Reims after Orléans
she would have taken him then. Had the Voices, after Patay,
whispered Paris, she would have let the coronation wait. Her

plan now was to go at once to Reims, then to Paris—not with
a dauphin, but with a king duly crowned and anointed. This
was her plan and much is to be said in its favor. Charles arriving
in Paris a crowned king, the Maid at his side, was a spectacle
that would speedily unite all France. The fighting would end,
English soldiers would return to England. To Joan the way
ahead seemed clear. She knew her people and her army; but
apparently neither Joan nor her Voices in that moment thought
of treachery.

The Maid and her army camped in and about Patay and next
day after dinner marched to Orléans. Expecting the King to
make it his starting point for Reims, the city had dressed its
streets for his welcome. But Charles, in the midst of pleasures
at La Trémouille's chateau at Sully, showed little interest in
Orléans, or in his coronation. The Maid rode to St.-Benoit and
to Sully, to carry the great news in person and to stir him to
action.

"Come to Reims, come to Reims and receive your crown!"
again she urged; and she implored him to accept and forgive
Richemont, who had rendered such good service at Patay and
would go with him to the coronation. Charles postponed the
start for Reims and while he promised to forgive Richemont he
refused on La Trémouille's account to receive him or to let him
join the coronation journey. Again, and a third time, Joan saw
the King and begged him to start for Reims.

"Doubt not," she said, "you will gain all your kingdom and
will soon be crowned."

Seeing that she was deeply troubled, Charles spoke to her
kindly and counseled her to rest after her battles, all of which
must have sounded like mockery to Joan, who only grew weary
of idleness and saw her precious days flying.

But presently, finding that most of the captains agreed with
Joan, the King went to Gien, whence the coronation journey
was to start. Joan, Alençon and the army also went to Gien
and began preparations for the march. At Gien she wrote a

letter to the people of Tournai inviting them to Reims, so sure
was she of arriving there. Also, she wrote to the Duke of Burgundy, begging him to lay aside enmity and render fealty to
the King at Reims. Again there were delays. Provisions for the
expedition were short and there was a scarcity of funds with
which to pay for them. Advice against starting was about the
only thing that was plentiful and certainly the prospect of
marching with a great force through an enemy country was
far from alluring.

Joan was impatient with the objectors. Her faith disregarded
all obstacles.

"By my staff," she said, "I will conduct the noble Charles
and his company safely and he will be crowned at the said place
of Reims!"

Captains and men were with her. They would give their
services to the King, they said, for this journey, and would go
wherever she would go. She left her lodgings in Gien and made
her camp with them in the field. Two days later—it was the
twenty-ninth of June, Saint Peter and Saint Paul's day—there
started from Gien one of the strangest expeditions in history,
a glittering pageant of twelve thousand—men-at-arms, nobles,
princes—setting out through an enemy country, without artillery, almost without provisions and funds, led by a girl of seventeen who was taking a king to receive his crown.

Brother Richard was something
of a prophet

The brave array wound across the valley of the
Loire and entered the woods, taking the direction of Auxerre.
Four months earlier Joan had secretly visited that city on her
journey to Chinon. Her plan now was to enter by siege and
assault. Arriving at the end of the third day, the army camped

under the great walls which loomed high and forbidding in the evening.

The Maid and her captains believed it would be no great matter to take the place but the King's wily counselor, La Tré-mouille, had a milder and, for himself, more profitable plan. La Trémouille was always for negotiation—at a price. In this case he received two thousand crowns, with a delivery to the army of provisions, on which terms he agreed to keep the place from being assailed. The provisions were welcome enough but the leaders, confident that they could have taken the town by as-sault and unwilling to leave this enemy stronghold behind them, were disappointed and indignant. They wrathfully discussed La Trémouille, agreeing that such a compromise would not occur again. Next morning they took up the march, the army with provisions for a few days. What an amount it must have taken for that great cavalcade! Doubters and grumblers in the ranks—and in every army there are always enough of these— began to make complaint and prophesy evil; they were being led into the wilderness to die! An old chronicler writes that the Maid was everywhere with words of encouragement and harmony.

She rode fully armored and spoke as wisely as any captain and when any outcry or alarm arose among the soldiers, she came, whether on foot or mounted, and gave heart and cour-age to all the others, admonishing them to keep good watch and guard: though in all else she was just a simple girl.

St.-Florentin was their next camp, a walled town which opened its gates to them; then the village of St.-Phal, from which the Maid sent a letter to the chief men of Troyes, a large city in English and Burgundian hands. She urged the citi-zens of Troyes to render obedience to Charles, their true and rightful King, and have no fear for their lives or possessions.

Otherwise, with the aid of God, the King would enter, regardless of all resistance. Charles also wrote, asking submission, promising to be a good king to them if they received him.

A day later the Maid and her army arrived under the walls of the city and went into camp. No answer had come to her letter. The chief men of Troyes, strongly Burgundian, vowed the most sacred oaths that they would never surrender to this Maid. In a hasty letter to Reims they called her: "A fool full of the devil," declaring they had thrown her letter into the fire.

They even made a show of arms. On the day of Joan's arrival the gates of the city suddenly opened to let out a sortie of five or six hundred English and Burgundians; but they showed little taste for battle with the Maid's soldiers and quickly scurried back again, to appear no more.

The citizens were now in a state of much alarm. They knew what had happened at the Tourelles and at Jargeau and that their defenses were certainly no better. They had written to Reims and to the Duke of Burgundy, but expected no help from either. Reims was even suspected of being ready to open its gates to the Maid's army. A wandering friar called Brother Richard, a mixture of preacher and prophet, then in Troyes, claimed to have knowledge that Reims would be delivered to the King.

But if Troyes was in a bad way Joan's great army was little better off. Already at Auxerre there had been a shortage of provisions. Little had been obtained at St.-Florentin, and still less at St.-Phal. If Troyes held out it was only a question of days until the glittering twelve thousand must scatter in search of food, leaving the King to return ignominiously whence he had come.

The siege could hardly have endured more than a single day but for certain earlier counsel of the Brother Richard already mentioned. Whatever else he was Brother Richard was something of a prophet. During the previous winter he had appeared in Troyes and neighboring towns and with other advice had exhorted the people to sow beans in preparation for one who would come.

"Sow, good people! Sow abundance of beans; for he who comes will come quickly." Such, we are told, were his words, the significance of which seemed now clearly shown. The King had come, and Joan, and with them a great army whose support in part was the ripening wheat, rubbed from the ear in the hand, but chiefly the succulent beans that made green the wide stretches of the fertile hillside. For whatever Brother Richard may have meant the people had taken him literally. They had sown beans with a vengeance, and but for them many of the Maid's soldiers would have died.

As it was there was much discontent among both soldiers and leaders. Six thousand were without bread for nearly a week. Many counseled the King to return, especially as the towns still before him were in enemy hands.

The King summoned his advisers to decide what should be done; Joan was not invited to attend. Regnault de Chartres, Archbishop of Reims, presiding, stated that the army, for several reasons, could not well remain longer before the city. For one thing there was very little food, with no supplies to be had. Furthermore, there was no money to pay for supplies and certainly it would be a very marvelous thing to take a strong city, armed and provisioned, without heavy artillery, there being no French town or fortress from which aid could be expected nearer than Gien, now a hundred miles behind them.

The archbishop dwelt on these things and prompted by the King asked the opinions of the others present. No one spoke encouragingly. The King, they said, had been refused admission to Auxerre, a place of fewer soldiers and poorer defenses. The general opinion seemed to be that the King and his army should turn back. Then at last a senior member of the council, Robert le Maçon, who at Loches had heard the Maid urge Charles to undertake the journey to Reims, rose to speak.

"It is my opinion," he said, "that we should send for Joan

the Maid, who being of the army might very well have something to say of profit to the King and his company. When the King set out on this undertaking it was not because of any great force of arms he had nor sums of money nor indeed because the journey seemed very likely to succeed. The King undertook this journey solely on the advice of the Maid, who steadily urged him to go to his coronation at Reims, saying he would find there little resistance and that this was the will of God. Now let Joan be sent for: if she counsels nothing further than has already been said then I agree with the others that the King and his army should return. Let Joan speak, she may say something that will lead the King to another conclusion."

The King assenting, Joan presently appeared among them and the case was laid before her by the archbishop. She listened to the end, then turned to the King.

"Noble Dauphin, will you believe what I tell you?" she asked.

"Joan, if you say something profitable and reasonable I will willingly believe it."

The timid and cautious Charles could seldom give a direct answer. Joan looked into the face of the wavering monarch.

"If I speak will I be believed?" she repeated. Charles answered uncertainly: "Yes, Joan—according to what you say."

Upon which Joan spoke out boldly.

"Noble Dauphin of France," she said, "if you will remain here before your city of Troyes, it will be within your domination within two days, whether through force or through love; and of this make no doubt."

There was a stir among the counselors. When Joan spoke in that way her words carried conviction.

"Joan," said the archbishop, "could we be certain of having it in six days we might well wait. But do you speak as you see?"

"Make no doubt of it."

The meeting came to a sudden end. Joan, with Alençon, at once went to prepare for an assault. The Maid on a courser, staff in hand, rode among the army and set knights and squires and all others of whatever rank to work carrying faggots, doors, tables and shutters from the houses of the suburbs, whatever was suitable for shelters and approaches during an attack. Dunois told of this and added: "She made such marvelous diligence as might have made a captain bred all his days to war."

He added that she set up her tent near the moat and herself worked with such an energy as no two or three of the most experienced soldiers could have equaled. Strong and tireless as she was, the Maid seemed exalted by a holy purpose. The bold city fathers who had sworn to defend the city to their deaths faltered in the face of that night spectacle of a white-armored figure shouting orders, working meantime like something more than human, in preparation for the assault at daybreak. They remembered Jargeau and forgot their oath. To quote Dunois: "She worked in suchwise that next morning the bishop and bur-gesses of Troyes made their submission to the King, shivering and trembling."

The delegation which came out to surrender the city was preceded by the friar, Brother Richard, himself considerably frightened. He had been sent to make sure that the Maid came not from Satan but from God. He advanced shakily, making the sign of the cross and sprinkling holy water. Joan, amused, said to him: "Approach boldly, I will not fly away."

The Maid entered the city riding at the King's side, carrying her banner. Brother Richard, whose prophecies had been veri-fied and whose beans had saved the army, found himself in high favor. He is said to have preached a sermon eulogizing the Maid and he promptly attached himself to her train.

In Troyes as elsewhere, the people, most of whom were loyal, flocked about the Maid, striving to touch her, holding up their children to see her, weeping in the joy of their deliverance. At the church that day she held an infant at the font for baptism, a favor sought of her by many mothers. By the terms of the surrender only the city yielded, the English and Burgundian soldiers being permitted to withdraw with their belongings. It did not occur to Joan that the latter might include their prisoners and when she saw them leading off a number of wretched French captives, she promptly stopped the procession and compelled Charles, out of his scanty purse, to ransom them at the rate of about a silver franc [today worth $25] each.

It was at Troyes that the hated treaty had been made by the terms of which the little son of Henry V of England could lay claim to the throne of France. Charles now had the satisfaction of gaining the city where he had been deprived of his birthright.

"I fear only treachery"

The surrender of Troyes opened the way to Reims. Châlons, the only important town between, was known to be friendly, while Reims, long under Burgundian rule, was believed ready to welcome the French King. Regnault de Chartres, archbishop of that city, who since his accession had never been able to enter the place, now wrote requiring the people to receive the King for his coronation.

The rest of the journey was little more than a march of triumph. Alençon's squire, Perceval de Cagny, who rode with that gleaming pageant under the July sun, wrote:

> And as the King passed along all the fortresses of the country came under his submission because the Maid always sent some of those who were under her standard to say at each of the fortresses to those within: "Surrender to the King of Heaven and to the noble King Charles." And these, having knowledge of the great marvels that had taken place in the presence of the Maid, all placed themselves freely in submission to the King. And to those who refused she went in person and all obeyed her. Sometimes on the way she rode with the main army with the King; at other times with the advance guard and again with the rear guard, as she found most suitable.

Arcis was the first town beyond Troyes but villages were not far apart and the road now was lined with adoring multitudes, oppressed and long-suffering people who in Joan saw an angel of God sent for their deliverance—many of them kneeling as she passed, bending forward to kiss or touch her hands, her armor, even her horse. She asked them not to do this, for it was worship which she would have prevented. She spoke words of comfort to them and their tears flowed as they listened. They had suffered so much and so long! She once said that the poor had come to her gladly, for the reason that she did not cause them unhappiness but sustained them as well as was in her power.

Two days after leaving Troyes, on the morning of July 14, Joan and the King with their great following rode into Châlons-sur-Marne. Among the swaying crowds there was a small group to whom the sight of Joan riding with the King was as a strange and splendid dream. These were friends and comrades from Domrémy who had traveled nearly a hundred miles, probably on foot, to see their former neighbor and playmate pass by in glory. One of them was her godfather, Jean Morel, and Durand Laxart may have been among them. Later they came to her or she and her brothers sought them out. With what awe those simple country folk regarded their former comrade who in a brief half year had risen to heights as far above them as the stars. To Jean Morel she made a present of a red dress she had worn, without doubt the patched skirt in which she had set out for Vaucouleurs. If only it might have been preserved!

Asked by one if she had no fears for the days ahead, she answered: "I fear only treachery."

It was not ordinary treachery that she meant, the betrayal of her person into the hands of the enemy, but treason that would betray the cause of France. Knowing the evil near the King she had come to realize this possibility.

XIII

REIMS

Another two days and the towers of Reims rose above the level horizon. A little to the eastward of that city is a rise of ground and from it Joan first saw the great cathedral loom dreamlike against the afternoon sky. Among the soldiers about her there was excitement and eager pointing and on every side the cheering multitude. Amid all this we may believe that the Maid herself uttered no audible word but only sat and gazed, seeing little for the happy tears. Then presently they were in the city, the street a tossing human river that bore them to the doors of their lodging place.

Joan may have known that her father was in that throng. Those whom she had met at Châlons could have told her he was on his way to the great spectacle, to see the daughter he had once threatened to drown now in the moment of her triumph, the greatest ever achieved by any woman of France. He was enormously proud of her, of course, and proud to be known as her father. He lodged just across from the cathedral and lost no time in seeking the presence of his soldier children.

There was to be no delay in the coronation. Nobody wished to delay it. The city did not care to feed the great army a day longer than was necessary, while Joan was eager to push on to Paris. It was on Saturday July 16 that the Maid and the King reached Reims and the great service was arranged for the next day. All through the night there was busy preparation that the city might show itself in readiness by daybreak. Streets were decorated with banners; festoons were hung where the King and the Maid and their escort of richly attired churchmen and nobles would pass; gay tapestries were suspended from the windows.

At an early hour next morning—it was Sunday, July 17, 1429 —four nobles, according to ancient custom, were sent to the abbey church of St.-Rémy, to escort from there the sacred Ampoule, a phial of holy oil believed to have been brought from Heaven by a dove for the consecration of Clovis more than nine hundred years before and since held sacred for the anointing of French kings. These nobles took the accustomed oath to conduct and reconduct the precious vessel safely, and fully armed and mounted, carrying each his banner, they accompanied the gorgeous procession of churchmen bearing it to the cathedral—rode their horses straight into the great church, to the entrance of the choir, almost to the very altar itself. All this we are told in a letter written to Queens Marie and Yolande by three gentlemen of Anjou, eyewitnesses of the event.

The King, the letter says, found all in complete submission to him at Reims and all the requirements for his coronation, such as robes, vestments and a crown, as fully provided as if they had been ordered a year before. "And there were so many persons as would be a thing without end to write and, as well, the great joy that each felt."

The letter then quaintly tells of the great lords present and

how Alençon knighted the King and how another lord held the sword while the Archbishop of Reims performed the ceremony of consecration:

> The which service lasted from nine o'clock until two. And at the hour that the King was anointed and also when the crown was placed on his head, all assembled cried out "Noël!" And the trumpets sounded in such manner that it seemed that the vaults of the church must be riven apart.
>
> And during the said mystery the Maid was ever near the King, holding her standard in her hand. And a most fair thing it was to see the beautiful bearing of the King and of the Maid. And God knows it was wished that you were there.

This is the only account of any eyewitness, but a chronicle of the time says that when the Maid saw the King anointed and crowned she knelt before him and embracing his knees said, the hot tears flowing: "Noble King, now is accomplished the pleasure of God, who willed that I should raise the siege of Orléans and should bring you to this city of Reims to receive your holy coronation, thus showing that you are the true King, him to whom the throne of France must belong."

It may well be so; something of the sort she would be moved to do. The great audience, we are told, wept with her. The peasant girl had made good her promise. They were witnessing an event without counterpart in human history.

Of Joan's appearance on this great occasion we know little. Her page, Louis de Contes, was present, perhaps by her very side; but he only said: "I attended the coronation. In my quality of page I never quit Joan."

That is all; and how much he might have told us! Mingling with such glories, bursting with pride, yet not a hint of the Maid's dress nor of what she did and said. We may picture her wearing her armor, over it the crimson *huque* given her by the Duke of Orléans. We know that her banner was there and by her own testimony that she held it, at least for a time. Did Louis de Contes stand by her side with the sacred sword of Fierbois? Oh, Louis de Contes, graceful, graceless picturebook boy! How we blame you and how we envy you—the most fortunate youth in history!

The only thing Joan ever asked of France

Of the great assembly that saw Joan's triumph there were at least six persons who felt in it a deep and especial pride: her two loyal knights, Jean de Metz and Bertrand de Poulengy; her two brothers; her father, Jacques d'Arc; and best of all loyal Durand Laxart, first to receive her confidence and join his faith to hers. As he stood there, his eyes wide with the splendor of it all, did he remember that winter morning on the frozen road beyond Greux when this strange girl, now the wonder and glory of France, had bade him ask Sire de Baudricourt to have her conducted to the King? He had believed in her; this was his reward.

Jacques d'Arc did not immediately return home and when he did, he went the proudest man in France. On the morning after the coronation, at Joan's request, Charles VII gave his royal promise that the heavily burdened villages of Domrémy and Greux should from that time be forever free of taxation, a promise later affirmed by official mandate, which made it as nearly eternal as any king's promise is ever likely to be. During more than three hundred and sixty years the tax books of the district bore after the names of Domrémy and Greux the words "*Néant, la Pucelle*" ("Nothing, the Maid"). Then came the Revolution and this modest grace, the only thing that Joan ever asked of France, was abolished. Tradition said that Charles had required her to name her reward and that she would accept only this. Certain it is that for herself she accepted nothing, received nothing, not even loyalty.

Jacques d'Arc remained in Reims until the official document came. The King on his own account had presented him with a purse of sixty francs—a large sum when one remembers that a horse could be bought for twelve. Nor was this all, for at last when he was ready to go the City Council voted to pay in full his bill at the inn and to present him with a horse on which to return home.

And so it happened that once upon a time a simple peasant who had walked a long way to see the King crowned went riding home on a fine horse, in his pocket not only a purse but a document that relieved his villages from taxation, made them unique among all the villages of France. No fairy tale was ever more wonderful.

XIV

CHARLES THE DELUDED

*Hypocrisy and treachery were
on every hand*

To many readers it may seem that Joan might
now have returned, if not to the peace of Domrémy, at least to
Orléans or Tours, where she would be held in love and honor,
while brave and capable captains concluded the work of driving the invader from France. More than once she declared that
she had little taste for battle, that she longed to be spinning by
her mother's side. Even historians have held that her mission was
fulfilled—that there was no longer a reason for her remaining in
the field.

Joan's work, however, was in nowise ended. Only her first
three labors had been completed. She had raised the siege of
Orléans, she had conquered the English, she had crowned the
King. But Paris, the French capital, was still in English hands;
the English were still in France, the Duke of Orléans remained

a prisoner in England. We know that she regarded the restoration of Duke Charles as a part of her purpose; also, that she proposed to take Paris and drive the English from French soil. The brief year allowed her would prove all too short.

It was the Maid's plan to march immediately upon Paris and in the beginning Charles must have agreed to do this. Such a move could not fail of success. Paris, poorly garrisoned, overawed by Joan's triumphs and with its defenses in bad repair, was still ready to open its gates. A three days' march and the King would have been in his capital. Everybody expected that move, everybody except La Trémouille, the Archbishop of Reims and the Duke of Burgundy. These three were hatching treachery, the one thing Joan had learned to fear. They were preparing for the stupid Charles a treaty which would delay the march on Paris until English troops could reach there and the fortifications could be repaired. Complete victory over the English did not suit La Trémouille and the archbishop—it would put an end to their trading industry. Their dealings through Burgundy, who held what might be called the balance of power, must have been highly profitable both for themselves and for the wily Burgundy.

Joan herself wished for peace with the Duke of Burgundy if he would separate himself from the English. Her letter written in June begging him to render fealty to Charles at Reims had brought no answer. On the morning of the coronation, however, she wrote again, urging him to "war no more on the holy kingdom of France," and to withdraw immediately from all the fortresses of the King. The letter was long and earnest. In one place she said: "I pray and beseech you with clasped hands no longer to battle or make war against us, neither you nor your people nor your subjects. And believe surely that whatever number of people you may lead against us, they will gain nothing and there will be great sorrow from the blood that will be shed by those who will come against us."

Burgundy paid no attention to this letter. He would have no dealings with Joan, whom he may have regarded as a witch.

Furthermore, his alliance with England still offered the best profit. He preferred to deal with Charles through La Trémouille. On the very day of the coronation his embassy arrived at Reims with secret proposals for a treaty, one that meant no more than the cessation of hostilities under the promise—a promise he never meant to keep—that Paris would be yielded at some specified time. Such treaties were not uncommon in that day but they generally came to nothing in the end, being mere excuses to enable one side or the other, or both, to prepare more leisurely for battle. In this case it was Burgundy and the English who needed the delay, and the weak Charles, brought by La Trémouille and the archbishop to think that if given time Paris would be his without battle, was persuaded to sign.

It is almost beyond belief but Charles, crowned and no longer in fear of capture or exile, gave little heed to Joan, allowing those two malign counselors to sway him as they chose. He did not leave Reims the day following his coronation nor the next day nor the next. It was on Sunday that he was crowned and it was not until Thursday that he finally left with the army, not for Paris but for Corbény, which lies seventeen miles in quite another direction. Here was performed the ceremony supposed to give the King power to cure scrofula by touching the patient. At another time there might have been some excuse for this but with the English hurrying reinforcements to Paris and madly strengthening the walls to withstand attack, this particular rite could have waited. Joan and her captains urged and implored the King to turn a deaf ear to his poisonous advisers and Burgundy's silly promises and march on Paris while there was yet time. Charles marched to Soissons instead, a step, it is true, in the right direction, but dazzled there by the surging throng and banners of welcome, with ears only for the shouts of "Noël!" and the sinister counsel of La Trémouille, he lingered on in that city a *full five days*, during which an English army of five thousand marched into Paris! The time for easy capture had passed.

Leaving Soissons, Charles and his army marched south. It was no longer Joan's army or Alençon's, for they no longer controlled it. Its movements were directed by Charles himself; that is to say, by La Trémouille. At Reims the Maid's star had reached its zenith: from the moment the crown was on the King's head her power had begun to decline. The change became noticeable: the next town, Château-Thierry, showed resistance, though at evening it surrendered. Three days later the King was again on the march and in another day was at Provins, heading, it seemed, toward the Loire.

There is, however, good reason for believing that he was only keeping his dwindling army fed while he waited for the time named in the treaty with Burgundy, fondly believing that Paris would be yielded as agreed. At all events, he did not continue his course to the south. One chronicler of the time says that an English detachment at Bray on the Seine compelled him to turn back. This does not sound true. The English were only too eager to get Charles and the Maid out of the region near Paris into the Loire country where the army would presently break up; moreover, no mere English detachment could have turned the army back had it wished to go on. Bedford was scouting around with his troops and wrote Charles a fiercely abusive letter, but he showed no disposition to fight and presently marched back to Paris.

Charles lingered at Provins a few days, then also turned in the direction of Paris, in the hope that somewhere about the fifteenth of August Burgundy would let him march in. The date of their treaty is unknown but being made toward the end of July it was probably drawn as of August 1, its terms being that Paris would be surrendered at the end of fifteen days. All that we know of it is from a letter written by Joan to the loyal French at Reims, who had become alarmed at the continued retirement of the King's army. In this letter Joan urges those of Reims to have faith in her, promising not to desert them *as long as she lives*. Of the treaty she writes: "It is true that the King has made a truce with the Duke of Burgundy . . . by which he must render the city of Paris at the end of fifteen days. Nevertheless, do not marvel if I do not enter so soon."

Joan knew the treaty for what it was, a mere excuse by which Burgundy and the English could gain time to prepare for defense. Not a soul but Charles himself had any faith in it. That La Trémouille and the archbishop had been paid for persuading the gullible King to sign it is as certain as anything can be without positive proof.

Joan's letter has in it a note of sadness. The great opportunity had gone by. She had been betrayed and she knew it. She was never the same after Reims. *"As long as I shall live"*—the words are significant. Her precious, limited weeks were racing by.

A few days later, when the army had moved still farther northward, and the people were running before the King and Joan, "transported with joy [it is Dunois speaking], crying 'Noël!' the Maid, riding between the Archbishop of Reims and myself, said: 'These are good people. I have seen none elsewhere who have shown so much joy at the coming of our noble King. Would God I might be happy enough, when I shall finish my days, to be buried in this soil!'

"At these words the archbishop said to her: 'Oh, Joan, in what place do you hope to die?'

" 'Wherever it may please God,' she replied. 'I am sure neither of the time nor the place. I know no more of it than yourself. But I would that it were pleasing to God, my Creator, that I might now retire, laying arms aside, and that I might serve my father and my mother, guarding their sheep with my sister and my brothers, who would be greatly rejoiced to see me!' "

Dunois may not have remembered Joan's exact words, but the feeling in them he must have preserved. She was tired. Lurking forces opposed her. Hypocrisy and treachery were on every hand. She yearned to leave it all, to rest again in the shade of the Fairy Tree, to hear once more the trickle of the cooling fountain. But because her work was still unfinished, because it could not be finished so long as knaves and traitors controlled the feeble King, because it was only just begun, she could not go.

The field of Montépilloy

Bedford in his violent letter to Charles had dared the King to meet him in the field, which may have opened Charles's eyes to the fact that Paris would not be surrendered. At all events he was now marching here and there, expecting to meet Bedford somewhere in the country just above Paris. The fifteen-day truce was about to expire. Did he imagine that Burgundy would find some way to keep faith or had he, for the moment at least, like Joan concluded that peace with Burgundy could be made "only at the point of the lance"?

At last, on Sunday the fourteenth of August, the two armies, each in number about six thousand, found themselves facing each other, a little to the eastward of the town of Senlis near the plains of Montépilloy. The French were camped along a hedge, while the English had their backs to a little stream. With Bedford were several hundred Burgundians, enough to claim that Charles had broken the truce if he attacked them. During the afternoon there was skirmishing in the open field between the armies, with loss on both sides. Next day came the battle, such as it was. Alençon's squire, De Cagny, wrote in his memoirs:

On Monday, fifteenth day of the said month of August, 1429, the Maid, the Duke of Alençon and the company, believing this day to have battle, each and all at whatever place made such peace as he could with his conscience and heard mass at the earliest hour possible, after which they took to horse. They formed their line of battle near that of the English, who had not moved from the place where they had camped and all night long had fortified themselves with *paulx*

[sharpened poles, planted point forward] and trenches, their wagons in front of them and having the river behind them.

Bedford had no intention of meeting Charles in the open. His army was entrenched behind a defense as strong as he could make it. He displayed the banner of France along with that of England, thus giving the French notice that Charles was an outlaw.

Seeing that the English would not come out into the open, the Maid placed herself at the head of the advance guard and led a charge even to their formidable defenses. This seems to have brought out a certain number of the English, for there was a skirmish during which men were killed on both sides. Joan had hoped to provoke a general battle. Failing in this, she withdrew her men and with Alençon sent a herald to the English, asking that they come forth and fight in the open, offering to give them time to range themselves in order of battle. This they would not do, though from time to time a venturesome party sallied forth, to be met by a party equally venturesome from the other side. These minor combats in the open made a gallant spectacle for the watching armies and in the course of them men were killed and wounded. Stirred by the sight, even La Trémouille was moved to join one of these brisk encounters and nearly came to grief. He was a very fat man and mounted on a beautiful courser, lance in hand, made an impressive figure. He may have been too heavy for his mount for at a critical moment his charger stumbled, pitching the fat knight into the midst of his enemies, where he barely escaped being killed or taken. Unhappily he was rescued and did not venture again.

The King from a safe place enjoyed this petty warfare which led to nothing and as night drew on retired to Crépy, eight miles behind the lines. Joan and Alençon camped with the army on the field. Nothing further happened and next morning it was found that the English had quietly taken the road back to Paris. There was no attempt to follow them; the Maid with the army joined the King at Crépy, where next day the keys of the important city of Compiègne were delivered to him.

One can hardly fail to note the change in Joan's warfare. Brave as ever, she was not the same. Distrust and treachery were taking the heart out of the Maid. She was no longer the shining white figure that at nightfall before the enemies' camp shouted fearsome warnings and next day swept the field with whirling charges led as by Saint Michael himself. The King was no longer with her; not only her soldiers felt this, but the enemy. She would still have great moments in the field but the Joan who had rallied her fleeting men at St.-Loup; who with La Hire had charged the Augustines; the Joan who, wounded, had led the last victorious charge against the Tourelles, who at Jargeau had been struck down only to spring to her feet shouting "Friends, up! up! Our Lord has condemned the English!"—that Joan led only in semblance on the field of Montépilloy.

XV

PARIS

"I wish to see Paris at closer range"

Compiègne was a strong town and Charles now
established himself there. Senlis, as soon as the English were
gone, offered submission; also Beauvais, from which retired the
Burgundian bishop Pierre Cauchon, nursing his wrath for a day
of fearful revenge. Other towns of Normandy and Picardy
submitted, and many more were ready to do so if only the King
would but take the trouble to visit them.

Charles in Compiègne, flattered and lulled by La Trémouille
and his kind, was satisfied with what had been done already.
He was tired with all this marching and fighting. Why must
Joan always keep on fighting? No other King had accomplished
so much in so short a time; why not rest and think it over? Besides, there was Burgundy, ready to make a new treaty. The
first had not been kept but that no doubt had been largely Joan's
fault. La Trémouille said so, and the archbishop, and they were

in a position to know. If Joan had not kept bothering Bedford, probably Burgundy would have surrendered Paris as agreed. This was about the way Charles reasoned, directed by his capable counselors. We sicken to think of Joan's high-hearted nobility wasted on one so paltry as Charles—for the moment, tragically enough, occupant of the throne of France.

At Compiègne the Maid once more took matters into her own hands; De Cagny writes that eight days after Montépilloy she called Alençon and said to him: *"Mon beau duc,* make ready your men and some other captains. By my staff, I wish to see Paris at closer range."

They prepared to leave at once and on August 23 marched out of Compiègne with a fine body of troops. Three days later they were at St.-Denis, near the gates of Paris. Bedford, now in Rouen, and Burgundy in Paris were alarmed. Burgundy hastily sent an emissary to the King to complete the new treaty.

The emissary had little trouble. Advised by La Trémouille and the archbishop, Charles within a week signed a treaty which gave Burgundy control of most of northern France in return for allowing Joan to attack Paris; the King himself remaining neutral, though from what followed it is clear that he had pledged himself to the Maid's failure. Charles, prompted by the archbishop, even tried to give Burgundy Compiègne, his best stronghold of the region, but the people of that city feared and hated the duke and in an open and formal protest refused to be given.

The Maid's troops, in camp at La Chapelle, skirmished about the gates of the capital while Joan and her captains daily considered the defenses and the best point of attack. They did not know that the King had pledged their defeat; they thought that if he would only come his presence would inspire the soldiers to deeds of valor. Urged by the Maid and Alençon the King did come a step nearer to Paris, as far as Senlis. Perhaps if he would write a letter to the citizens such as he had written at Troyes, the gates might even be opened without assault. The greater number in Paris were loyal or could easily become so. The King's presence before the gates might be all that was needed. Alençon went to Senlis and urged him to come to St.-Denis. The pusillanimous Charles promised, but did not come. Alençon went again and this time spoke so vigorously that Charles actually started, and on Wednesday September 7 was at dinner at St.-Denis, to the great joy of the Maid and also of the army, who said: "She will put the King inside Paris if it only depends on her."

The white armor laid aside

Joan did not wait for Charles to run away. With all her force and with such preparation as had been made, she attacked next day the walls of Paris. She confessed later that she had not been ordered by her Voices to make the assault and that her captains had only intended a demonstration of arms, but that it was her intention to pass the moats—that is, to attack the walls. Moreover, it was the day of the Virgin's nativity, unsanctioned as a day of battle. That Joan would make such an assault shows the desperate state of her mind. The King was not on the field but he was as close as he was ever likely to be. His coming had given the army a kind of confidence. It was now or never.

The attack began in the early afternoon at the Porte St.-Honoré. There were two moats outside the walls, the outer one empty, the other full of water. Joan with her standard, followed by her captains and soldiers, the latter with a quantity of scaling material, advanced to the dry moat. Looking up to those on the walls the Maid called out: "Surrender to the King of France!"

The answer was a flight of arrows; the Maid and her men descended into the ditch, crossed it and the space beyond, dragging bundles of wood and faggots to fling into the water-filled moat next the walls. Meantime the cannons had opened, flinging stone balls among them, while arrows, darts and javelins rained from the parapets. De Cagny, who was present, wrote: "The assault was severe and long and it was marvelous to hear the noises of the cannons and muskets that those within directed on those without, and from all manner of shafts so thickly planted as to seem innumerable."

Unknown to those without, friends of the King had started an alarm within the walls, shouting that all was lost, hoping to create a panic in the midst of which the gates would be opened. Many ran to their homes and barred the doors but the outcry produced no other effect. According to De Cagny, though many of the Maid's soldiers were struck their wounds were not serious. He thinks that none were killed but this is probably a mistake. In any case Joan's men could not cross the water moat though they brought a great quantity of filling material and worked until sunset of that long September day. Even then the Maid refused to give up the attack. She thought there must be a place where the water was less deep that they could fill and so get their scaling ladders across and against the walls.

But then came the end. According to one account, she stood calmly testing the depth of the moat with a lance when a shaft fired from above pierced her thigh, even as her shoulder had been pierced at Tourelles. She fell but refused to be carried from the field. De Cagny writes:

And after she was struck, she insisted more strongly than ever that the soldiers should attack the walls and that the place would be taken. But because it was nightfall and she was wounded and because the soldiers were weary with the long assault they had made, the Sire de Gaucourt and others came to take the Maid and against her wish carried her from the moats.

And thus failed the assault. And she had very great regret thus to depart, saying: "By my staff, the place would have been taken!"

They placed her on a horse and conducted her to her lodgings at La Chapelle, this time wounded body and soul, for she had met defeat.

Wounds seemed to have troubled Joan little. Next morning, sending for Alençon, she begged him to have the trumpets sounded for an assault on Paris, saying she would never leave until she had the city.

The prospect of taking the capital could not have been wholly discouraging, for Alençon and some of the other leaders favored her proposal to return. While they were discussing, the Baron of Montmorency, heretofore with the Burgundians, arrived with reinforcements for the Maid. This was encouraging; a hearty and determined assault might still win.

It was not undertaken. A message from the King commanded Alençon and other captains to appear before him at St.-Denis, bringing the Maid with them. They obeyed unwillingly enough for they believed it meant the end of any action for that day. Alençon had caused a bridge to be built across the Seine near St.-Denis; their hope now was to cross it and attack Paris from the other side.

Charles did put an end to action for that day. Nor was that all, for next morning when the Maid, Alençon and others determined to cross the Seine and attack Paris from another point they found that during the night the King had *caused the bridge to be destroyed!*

It was now all too clear how completely Charles had been delivered to Burgundy. The treachery which Joan had mentioned at Châlons and more than suspected at Reims, was complete; the cause of France had been sold like merchandise. As for Joan herself, if she had been lured into a wilderness and struck down she could not have been more deliberately or basely betrayed. What did she think of it all? What did she say to the King? We shall never know.

Charles, rejoicing in the thought that he had a long truce with Burgundy—it was to last until Christmas—was in haste to get to his castles on the Loire where he could enjoy it. The Maid now could not constantly be urging him to march against cities. Why attack Paris, anyway? It was no winter residence for a King. For two days he discussed these things, "tending always toward returning to the Loire," says De Cagny, "to the great affliction of the Maid." On the third day he made ready to depart. Joan's Voices having told her to remain at St.-Denis, she went all the more unwillingly.

And before going she had her white armor brought and gazing upon it knew that she would never wear it again. How proud she had been to see it grow under the deft hands of the workmen at Tours! Battle had dented and stained it since then: the patch on the shoulder was from the day before the Tourelles, the dent in the helmet was from a stone at Jargeau, the freshly pierced plate in the *cuissard* told of her failure before Paris.

"Take it to the church," she said.

They carried it to the church and with her own hands she laid it, with her sword, upon the altar. Then because she had been wounded and because these had been the arms of victory and could not remain the arms of defeat, kneeling she offered them to Saint Denis, whose name was the war cry of France.

XVI

BACK TO THE LOIRE

"And thus was broken the will of the Maid"

The spectacle of Joan laying her armor on the altar of Saint Denis meant little to Charles, whose one thought was to get back to the Loire, to ease and security. In his view the Maid had done all the important things; she should be glad now to rest and get over her wounds. "So he was off," wrote De Cagny, "taking with him the Maid, who with very great regret went in company with the King, who left as fast as he could go, pursuing his course in a manner disorderly and without cause."

The army was no longer the brave pageant that had left Gien two months earlier. It was a straggling, dwindling assortment held together by the Maid, Alençon, Dunois and a few other hardy leaders. Many captains with their soldiers had returned to the towns of their command and each day saw others ride away.

Whatever may have happened before, nobody this time attempted to turn the army back. Nothing occurred until it reached the river Yonne, which it expected to cross by the bridge at Sens. But the people of Sens, observing the size and condition of the army and being of uncertain mind, closed their gates, and it was humbly obliged to ford the river below the town. From there the distance was not great to Gien, where it finally arrived September 21, 1429.

"And thus," concludes De Cagny, "was broken the will of the Maid and the army of the King."

At Gien the remains of the army disbanded. Alençon, safe and sound as Joan had promised, returned to his wife and domain at Beaumont, where he soon assembled men to enter Normandy against the English. Realizing what her presence would mean, he sent to the King asking for the Maid, a request which Charles was not permitted to grant.

Taking Joan himself, the King now went to his old capital, Bourges, where the Queen awaited him. At Bourges, Joan lodged in the house of a worthy woman, Margaret la Touroulde, whose husband managed the royal finances, such as they were. During the three weeks that Joan remained with Madame la Touroulde persons of every rank came to see her, many of them with objects which they wished her to touch to render them fortunate or healing. Joan, amused, said: "Touch them yourselves. They will be quite as good with your touch as mine."

Madame la Touroulde said to her: "If you are not afraid to make assaults it is because you well know that you will not be killed."

Joan answered: "I am no more sure of that than are the soldiers."

"Joan was very liberal in almsgiving," Madame la Touroulde testified, "and with good will helped the poor and indigent, saying: 'I have been sent for the consolation of the needy.' From what I know of her she was simple and innocent except in the matter of arms. She mounted a horse and handled a lance like the best."

"Faggots and brush, everybody!"

Joan could not long remain in idleness. Half of her precious year was gone and so much yet to be done! The English were still in Paris, in Normandy and Picardy—they were even in two places below Orléans: La Charité on the Loire and St.-Pierre-le-Moutier, forty miles to the southeast of Bourges. It was Joan's wish to go into the country near Paris and reduce the capital by cutting off its supplies. The new truce with Burgundy prevented this. It would not expire till Christmas and was later extended till Easter. La Trémouille and Charles did not find it pleasant to have Joan about, always urging action, so gave her permission to drive the English from these two towns. They were not covered by the truce; if Joan could amuse herself attacking them, so much the better. A little warfare going on always afforded a chance for La Trémouille to pick up profits for himself. He replaced Alençon with his own half brother, D'Albret, the Maid and D'Albret being equal in command. Their army was too small and too poorly supplied, but they marched on St.-Pierre and began the siege. An assault being ordered, the soldiers attacked with good will but the place was well defended and they were obliged to fall back. D'Aulon, who had been wounded in the heel and was limping about on crutches, noticed that Joan with her brothers and knights did not retire with the others. Hastily mounting a horse, he rode up to them.

"Why are you staying here?" he demanded. "You are alone."

But the Maid, lifting the casque of her helmet, shouted: "We are not alone! I have with me fifty thousand of my people and will not leave this place until I have taken the town!"

D'Aulon stared. There were no more than four or five in her company, as he said later.

"Come away from here," he entreated, but Joan answered: "Have men bring faggots and brush and make a bridge across the moat," and herself called out loudly: "Faggots and brush, everybody! to make a bridge."

And suddenly the men were there again, building the bridge and, in a twinkling as it seemed, scaling the walls. D'Aulon, who told of this, said he looked on amazed and that "immediately the town was taken without much resistance."

Here once again we have the real Joan. With the sanction and support of the King at Paris, "fifty thousand of her people" might have rallied there also.

The capture of St.-Pierre-le-Moutier occurred the first week in November. A few days later Joan at Moulins wrote to different towns for money and supplies to aid in the siege of La Charité. She was short of nearly everything and the King made no effort to replenish her stores. Some of the towns sent help, such as they could afford. One town, Clermont-Ferrand, besides other things, sent a sword, two daggers and a battle-ax, for Joan herself. Orléans sent clothing for the men, with guns, gunners and some money. Bourges also sent money, thirteen hundred écus of silver or gold, but it went by way of La Trémouille and unaccountably disappeared.

About all we know of the siege of La Charité is that it failed. The place was strongly fortified and the wide river that washed the walls of the town added to the Maid's problem. To attempt the capture of such a place in wintertime with an army too few in numbers, too poorly armed, ill fed and ill clothed, was about as hopeless an undertaking as can be imagined. To capture it by assault would have been a miracle greater than that of St.-Pierre-le-Moutier. When supplies failed entirely and no help of any sort was coming from the King, the Maid and D'Albret with great reluctance abandoned the siege and returned to Bourges.

The success or failure of La Charité was a matter of small moment to the King. As long as the English garrison there could work him no personal damage he cared little for what it might do to near-by villages. In his great castle at Mehun-sur-Yèvre he made Joan welcome; when she complained of the failure to send her supplies he executed a document which named her "dear and beloved" and conferred nobility not only on Joan but on her entire family of whatever kinship or lineage. By a penstroke Joan's parents had acquired nobility; her brothers could ride on equal terms with those of lofty birth. They took the name "Du Lys," with the armorial bearings which earlier in the year the King himself had designed for Joan's banner; the device of a sword supporting a crown, a fleur-de-lis on either side. Today we can hardly measure what this meant to Jean and Pierre d'Arc. The difference in the early fifteenth century between a peasant and a noble was about the difference between a barnyard fowl and an eagle. Joan herself cared very little for such honors. She seems never to have made use of her bearings. The King granted them without her request, she said, to give her brothers pleasure.

The Maid was now dragged about with the court, sometimes held at Mehun-sur-Yèvre, sometimes at Bourges, often at La Trémouille's great château at Sully. As a normal girl she might have enjoyed a reasonable diversion between victories; but with defeat just behind and no promise of conquest ahead, it was a vain and sickening show, a waste of her flying days.

Word came of the approaching marriage of Héliote Poulvoir, daughter of the artist at Tours who had decorated the Maid's banner. Remembering their happy days together and how grateful Tours had been for relief from the English menace, Joan wrote asking that the city vote one hundred écus with which to buy Héliote's trousseau.

Tours considered this request from the "beloved Maid" and declined to grant it. The city fathers decided instead to honor Héliote by attending her wedding and to furnish some bread and wine for the occasion. The incident is a rather sad one, indicating as it does Joan's waning prestige. Six months earlier a request from the Maid would have been more sacredly honored than an order from the King.

Orléans had not yet forgotten; at this very moment that city was lavishly entertaining the Maid, her household and several distinguished friends. But then Tours had not been besieged.

XVII

THE MAID'S LAST CAMPAIGN

The "flight from Sully"

Bad news arrived. The country to the north that had submitted to the King was again beset by English and Burgundian raiders; towns were captured and sacked; fields were deserted. Charles sent promises of aid, and a small force under De Boussac. La Hire was already fighting in Normandy, also Alençon and the Constable; the devastated country and endangered cities were farther to the eastward; Troyes and Châlons were threatened, even Reims. The Maid's work was going to wreck, while she herself was being trailed about after an idle and dissolute court.

It was near the middle of March when a letter came to her from Reims, telling of their situation, their fear of attack and siege. From Sully, Joan replied that she would be with them soon and if the enemy were there would "make them put on their spurs so quick that they would not know where to find them." She spoke of having good news. This was on March 16, 1430.

The Maid was now steadily urging the King to give her men and let her hasten to the rescue of the northern towns. Charles may have been holding her off until Easter (April 23), when the new truce with Burgundy would expire. In any case she was still in Sully twelve days later, for she wrote from there a second letter to Reims, assuring the city that the King knew of their troubles (reported plots to admit the Burgundians) and would send help "the very soonest" that he could. She asked them to keep close watch and guard, and again spoke of good news.

What then happened at Sully we shall never know, but a few days later, with or without the King's knowledge and sanction, Joan with a little band of followers left the Loire behind her forever. Charles may have known of her going and given her a few soldiers and a little money. She had become to him as a prodding conscience; he would be glad enough to be rid of her so that he could take his pleasure more peacefully. If he did not wish to violate his empty treaty with Burgundy she could seem to go secretly, "making semblance of going on some other diversion." According to one chronicler, she did this; for which reason her departure has been called the "flight from Sully."

On the moats of Melun

Of those who started with Joan we can only be sure of D'Aulon, her two brothers and Father Pasquerel. Did she have her two knights, gallant Jean de Metz and Bertrand de Poulengy, who on a winter evening a little more than a year before had ridden with her through the Porte de France? One likes to think of them being with her in this new adventure. Dunois, La Hire, Alençon—all these were gone. She may have had as many as fifty or as few as five. She rode northward, toward Lagny on the Marne, "because those of that place made good war on the English of Paris and elsewhere."

The Maid found welcome and plenty of soldiers at Lagny. Then a little farther and she was in the field, facing English and Burgundians ranged against a hedge. In the fight that followed she was victorious, the English and Burgundians being killed or captured.

For a time the Maid's headquarters remained at Lagny and a curious incident happened there. An infant who had died without baptism was brought to the church for prayer. A number of young girls had assembled and Joan was asked to pray with them that God and the Virgin would give the infant life. She went and prayed with the others. Finally, it was said, the child showed signs of life, upon which it was baptized, but presently died and was buried in holy ground. Joan herself told of this miracle but added that she was with the others on her knees at the time, saying her prayers. Being on her knees in prayer, surrounded by a throng, she could hardly have seen the miracle herself. What really happened we cannot know; but the excited young girls crowding about, their imaginations quickened by the fervor of their faith, may honestly enough have believed what they were eager to believe and to see.

Joan's movements here become uncertain. De Cagny was no longer with her to keep his faithful report. From herself we know that during Easter week (April 17–23) she was at Melun, twenty miles south of Lagny, and that she received there her first definite warning of her closing period of usefulness. Melun had been long in English hands but yielded to the Maid without much resistance. It was before the surrender that the warning came. Joan, telling of it, said: "During the week of last Easter, on the moats of Melun, I was told by my Voices, that is to say, Saint Catherine and Saint Margaret, that I would be captured before Saint John's Day and that it was necessary that this should happen and that I must not be astonished and must accept it willingly and that God would aid me."

She had never known what the end would be, doubtless hoping to die gloriously in battle. Now at last, in a moment of action and success, had come the warning. The year, the brief year allotted for her task, was at its close. She was not to be killed; she was to be captured!

A hundred times the English had promised her death by fire —no idle threat, as she well knew. Her Voices did not name the day nor the hour, though she asked them to do this, begging that when she should be taken she might die soon, without long suffering in prison. She confessed that if she had known the time she would not have gone into battle—at least not willingly.

"Nevertheless, I would have obeyed the command in the end, whatever the outcome."

A land picked clean by war

We know something of Joan's movements during the month that now followed, but the details are meager enough. She was once at Senlis with a thousand mounted men, and during the second week in May was at Compiègne, where she found the Archbishop of Reims, certainly there for no good purpose. Very likely he was trying to get the town to surrender to Burgundy, a thing he had done his best to accomplish the previous autumn. Burgundy's forces were now getting ready to lay siege; the archbishop's presence there has a suspicious look.

All about, there was fighting again. Joan's old comrade, Poton Saintrailles, was attacking the besiegers at near-by Choisy, a hopeless task. Joan, arriving at Compiègne, joined forces with Poton and together they rode fifteen miles north to cut off Noyon at Pont l'Evêque. There was a sharp engagement, then the enemy received help from Noyon and the Maid and Poton were obliged to retreat. Choisy surrendered to the Anglo-Burgundians, who now took up strong positions across the Oise, facing Compiègne itself.

Prospects for that city were not bright. It was poorly provisioned and while it had access to the country behind it, it was to a land picked clean by war. Hoping to attack the enemy in the rear, Joan led her force twenty-five miles east to Soissons to find a crossing. But Soissons was commanded by a Picard traitor, who at that moment was plotting with Burgundy to deliver to him the town. On the arrival of the Maid's army he ordered the gates closed, giving the excuse that he had no food for it, that the citizens would not permit its entry. Joan and her soldiers slept that night in the fields. Recalling the Soissons of ten months earlier, when the town had opened its gates to the Maid and her King and swarmed about them with glad cries of "Noël!" we realize the change that had come over this friendly people through the dallying of the incredible Charles. It was at Soissons that he had missed the last great opportunity to take Paris. Later neglect had estranged the town itself.

The country was too poor to support the Maid's army. They were without supplies, without plans. Captains with their companies drifted away. Joan with a small force, a few hundred at most, went to Crépy-en-Valois, hardly knowing what to do next. Whether by command of her Voices or of her own will, a few days later she decided to render such aid as she could to Compiègne.

Just after midnight on the twenty-third of May, 1430, with a company of three or four hundred, among them D'Aulon, her brothers and Pasquerel, the Maid rode out of the gates of Crépy. It was the dawn of the last day of her year—her year and a little more—of usefulness. She had no warning of it. When some of her people said that she had but few soldiers to go among the English and Burgundians she answered: "By my staff, we are enough! I will go to my good friends of Compiègne."

"Have no other thought than to strike"

At Compiègne Joan found that the enemy had established three camps across the river. One of these was the Burgundian camp of John of Luxemburg, two miles above Compiègne at the village of Clairoix. Another, an English camp, was less than a mile down the river, at Venette. The third camp was just opposite Compiègne at Margny, a village at the end of the bridge over the Oise.

Joan, with Guillaume de Flavy, governor of the city, agreed that this third camp should be destroyed. The Maid would lead a swift charge across the bridge, do as much damage as was possible in a brief time, her return to be protected by De Flavy with archers and muskets ranged along the city walls and the banks below. It was believed that the attacking party could break up the Margny camp and get back across the bridge before the enemy at Clairoix and Venette could be alarmed. It really seemed easy enough and about five o'clock, all being ready, the Maid with her banner at the head of five hundred men rode from the city gates. Over her armor she wore a crimson, gold-embroidered *huque,* doubtless the one given her by the Duke of Orléans, and so in fine attire entered her last battle for France.

Led by this brilliant figure the steel-clad company swept upon the drawbridge, crossed the river and a moment later struck the Burgundian camp. The attack was a surprise and in the beginning successful. It would have been all over in a few minutes had it not been that John of Luxemburg and some gentlemen of his company were just then riding from Clairoix to Margny, and had reached a point at the overhanging cliff where they could see what was going on. In hot haste word was sent back to Clairoix and in a very brief time groups of Burgundians were hurrying to the rescue of the attacked camp, while another cry of "To arms!" had somehow reached the English camp at Venette.

Joan and her company could easily have retreated by the bridge but their fighting blood was up. They met the arriving troops from Clairoix and drove them back in a succession of charges, only to find their own retreat cut off from behind by the English—five hundred strong, according to a Burgundian historian who was present.

"The French," he wrote, "seeing their enemies multiplying in great number, retreated toward their city, always the Maid with them behind the others, making a great effort to support her men and withdraw them without loss."

Thus does an enemy picture Joan in her last battle. "Remaining behind as chief and the most valiant of her band," wrote another, also a Burgundian. D'Aulon and Joan's brothers urged her toward the bridge.

"Make haste back to the town or we are lost!" they shouted, but she answered fiercely: "Be silent! it rests with you to defeat them! Have no other thought than to strike!"

This is the Joan of St.-Pierre-le-Moutier. Perhaps again she expected reinforcements from the sky. Those about her only pressed toward the bridge, dragging her with them.

Then all around them swarmed the enemy, in a frenzy to capture the French witch. There was a crush at the bridge entrance, soldiers crowding and slashing their way across it in a mass, the enemy pushing in from every side. De Flavy from the wall seeing this and fearing, as he claimed later, that the enemy would force through the gates, ordered the drawbridge raised. Those left without were doomed.

On that side of the river the ground was low and wet. A causeway, called a *boulevard*, ran out into the meadows and another along the river bank. On this raised ground Joan and those about her made their last stand: fierce, brief and hopeless. They were forced from the embankment into the wet meadows.

From every side hands clutched at the Maid. One of John of Luxemburg's men, an archer, caught the crimson and gold *huque* and dragged her from her horse. The others were obliged to yield. Some words were exchanged but it is uncertain what they were. Joan, her two brothers, with D'Aulon, faithful to the last and a brother of D'Aulon's, were borne off prisoners, the "good friends of Compiègne" looking on.[1]

---

1. It has been said that De Flavy deliberately betrayed Joan into English and Burgundian hands. De Flavy was a brave soldier but his personal record shows that he was capable of any crime. Moreover, he was a relative of the Archbishop of Reims and a deputy of La Trémouille, facts certainly not in his favor.

XVIII

CAPTIVITY

Charles was quite undisturbed

Joan was taken to the Burgundian camp at Clairoix, her captors shouting, dancing and embracing each other, more joyous over their capture, says the Burgundian chronicler, "than if they had taken five hundred men; for they neither feared nor dreaded any captain or commander so much as they had this Maid."

The Duke of Burgundy had his camp a distance away but he presently arrived to make sure that their prisoner was in truth the dreaded Maid. Joan and the duke spoke together but their words are lost.

The archer who had captured Joan was not permitted to hold her. She was too great a prize for that. His overlord, John of Luxemburg, promptly claimed her and a day or two later took her for safety to his castle of Beaulieu, about twenty miles from Compiègne to the northward. Her brothers may have gone with her; at all events D'Aulon did and was allowed to serve as her attendant.

Meantime, the news of Joan's capture flew in every direction throughout Europe. It reached the Archbishop of Reims, who justified it, charging Joan with being willful, unwilling to listen to advice, meaning his own advice and that of La Trémouille. God had suffered the capture of the Maid, he said, because of her pride and the rich raiment she had worn and because she had not followed God's commands but her own will. He forgot to mention that he and La Trémouille had been the means of preventing her, after the coronation, from marching at once upon Paris as she had planned.

The news reached Paris, where in celebration Bedford ordered *Te Deums* sung in all the churches and the University of Paris took immediate steps to get Joan into its hands for trial, delegating her deadliest enemy, Pierre Cauchon, Bishop of Beauvais, expelled from that city when it surrendered to Charles and the Maid, to bring the witch to justice.

It reached Charles along with the news of Compiègne, and the King sent word that he would aid the city, which of course he never meant to do, for as we know he had already done his best to deliver it to Burgundy. Of Joan he said nothing whatever. If he expressed any word of regret there is no trace or memory of it today. When the great churchman, the Archbishop of Embrun, who a year before had called Joan "an angel of the armies of the Lord," wrote him: "For the recovery of this girl and for the ransom of her life I bid you spare neither means nor money unless you would incur the indelible shame of disgraceful ingratitude," Charles was quite undisturbed at the prospect of shame and did nothing whatever. He was through with Joan. He had his crown and his cities on the Loire; he was no longer in personal danger. The Maid's eagerness always to be in action had annoyed him.

Knowing Charles, one is not much surprised at his indifference. Harder to understand is the attitude of Joan's old comrades, those who had fought by her side. One and all, they seemed to have accepted her capture as a part of the fortunes of war. We hear nothing of any sorrow, any plan for her rescue or ransom. A united effort might have accomplished one of these things. Joan was a prisoner of war; under the rules of that day she could possibly have been ransomed from John of Luxemburg, who was a free lance, poor and greedy, ready to sell the Maid like so much merchandise to the highest bidder. Orléans knew this, Tours knew it and on the news of Joan's capture, both these cities formed processions in which barefooted priests marched through the streets carrying images and praying for the Maid's deliverance, but they raised not a single sou with which to buy her life. Probably Bedford would have outbid any offer of theirs but it would be comforting today to know that they made one.

Never a fringe of lances on the horizon

The castle of Beaulieu, where Joan was imprisoned, was a brick affair, brick being much used in Picardy to this day. It was a strong dwelling rather than a gloomy fortress and Joan appears not to have been very closely confined. We really know little of her life there beyond the fact that she once came near escaping, "between two pieces of wood," as she said, probably slats or temporary bars of some sort of pen or across a window. She added that she would have shut her guards in the tower if it had not been for the porter, who saw and met her. We can only try to surmise what took place, and where D'Aulon was at the moment.

Joan could not know that she had been abandoned. She could not help believing that some of her former comrades would be lurking about, that once outside the walls she would fall into their hands. It would be hard for her to realize that no attempt was being made to save her who less than a year before had been the idol of France. A rumor was afloat that Charles had sent word to Burgundy that if anything happened to the Maid he

would take vengeance on such of the duke's people as fell into
his hands. This rumor may have reached Joan and given her
heart.

Nothing came of it. The Maid from her tower saw the level
fields grow red with poppies, but never a gleam of armor, never
a fringe of lances on the horizon. June brought the anniversaries
of Jargeau, of Beaugency and Patay. July brought the day of
the coronation when she had given the King his crown. That
had been a year ago, too short a time in which to be forgotten.
Surely she would be ransomed—the messengers with the news
might come any time.

D'Aulon was gloomy as to the general outlook. Once he said
to her: "That poor city of Compiègne which you most loved
will now again be placed in the hands of the enemies of France."
But she answered: "No, it will not; for the places that the King
of Heaven has reduced and restored to the hand and obedience
of the noble King Charles by means of me will never be retaken
by his enemies so long as he will use diligence to keep them."

The Maid's stay at Beaulieu came to an end. Some rumor of
a plan for her rescue or the eagerness of the Church to possess
itself of her caused her captor to remove her to the castle of
Beaurevoir some forty miles to the northeast, south of Cambrai.
D'Aulon seems to have been left behind, for we do not hear of
him again. He was the last link with her glorious year. She was
alone now in the hands of her enemies.

Beaurevoir was the home castle of John of Luxemburg and
Joan was not without female companionship. Luxemburg's aunt
Jeanne was there, a very old lady; also his wife and her daughter
by a former marriage—all, as it happened, of the same name. The
four Jeannes, or Joans, got on very well. The ladies of Beaurevoir
visited with the Maid of Domrémy and became fond of her.
Being orthodox, they urged her to lay off man's dress.

"Joan," said the aged demoiselle of Luxemburg, "we will give
you cloth for a woman's garment." The Maid shook her head
sadly.

"I would do it for you sooner than for any in France," she said, "except only for my Queen. But first I must have permission from God."

A young Burgundian knight, Aimond de Macy, was at the castle, doubtless in charge of the guards, for he came to know and admire Joan and gave some part of his time to her entertainment. But when he offered too gallant attention he found her deeply offended. He told this himself, adding: "My belief is that Joan is in paradise."

The one desperate chance

The University of Paris, controlled by the Burgundian branch of the Church and therefore by the English, from the start had been determined to have Joan, to try as a heretic and a witch. When the news came of her capture, the university wrote to the Duke of Burgundy and to John of Luxemburg humble, servile letters, naming Joan's offenses, offering her captors glories in this world and the next if they would deliver their prisoner to them—that is, to Pierre Cauchon, Bishop of Beauvais—for trial. Burgundy paid no attention to these letters, while John of Luxemburg plainly let it be known that he would not deliver Joan on the promise of glory in the hereafter but only for money paid in hand.

Bedford, regent for the English King, was behind the university. He intended to possess himself of Joan, as a prisoner not of war but of the Church. He meant to kill her. But it must be done in a way that would put a blemish on Charles's title to the crown. The Church would try her as a heretic, a blasphemer and a witch. Such a trial meant conviction and conviction meant the stake. That was Bedford's idea: to have Joan burned as a witch. Charles's crown, acquired through witchcraft, would thus become no crown at all. His title to it would be destroyed. Bedford's little nephew Henry VI, duly crowned and anointed, would be the king. Such was Bedford's idea; such his plan.

Pierre Cauchon, selected by the university to secure Joan and bring her to trial, was highly pleased with his assignment. Not only had the Maid been the cause of his exile from Beauvais, but it had been suggested that if he would bring about her conviction as a witch he would be made Archbishop of Rouen. To show his right to act as her judge, he promptly claimed that the Maid had been captured within the limits of his territory as Bishop of Beauvais, which was not true, Margny being in the bishopric of Soissons. No matter; with the English and Burgundian armies behind him Cauchon could claim anything.

Cauchon was a churchman of high standing but he knew a better way of getting Joan from John or Burgundy than by promising them treasures in heaven. The university had written again more fulsomely, more abjectly than before, but with the same result. Cauchon took ten thousand francs which Bedford had wrung from the people of Normandy in the form of a special tax and visited John in person, first in his camp at Compiègne, then at Beaurevoir, where Joan was held. Ten thousand francs, in that day a very large sum [today equal to $250,000], was the legal ransom of a prince or king. John was in no hurry to take it, perhaps hoping the other side would offer more. Lacking money, Charles might yield a good town, even a province. It was not easy to believe that the King of France would offer nothing for the Maid who had secured him his dominion and his crown.

Joan well knew what was going on. She knew when Cauchon came to Beaurevoir and how John's aged aunt had pleaded with her nephew not to sell his prisoner to the English. She knew that in spite of this plea she had been sold. Furthermore, she and all there knew that to be sold to the English was to be delivered to the flames.

With all this, news came that Compiègne would fall and that all in the town over the age of seven would be slain. Joan, beside herself, desperately resolved on another attempt of escape.

There was but one possible way. In the thick wall of her tower was a narrow slit which served as a window. It was not barred and she could squeeze herself through it. She knew that the ground was far below; the fall would probably kill her but in her desperate state of mind she had little wish to live. "I preferred to die," are her words, "rather than live after the destruction of these worthy people."

Desperate indeed she must have been, when to risk death in that way was a deadly sin. She knew this, for daily she discussed the matter with her Voices. Saint Catherine told her that she should not jump; that God would aid her, also those at Compiègne. The Voice said that she would not be delivered until she had seen the King of England. But Joan answered: "Truly, I have no wish to see him. I would rather die than be in English hands!"

Later Joan explained that she had not wished to kill herself, her hope having been to save her body and go to the rescue of those in Compiègne. Her Voices several times forbade her to jump but she could not control herself and at last, commending herself to God and the Virgin, she pushed through the narrow opening and leaped, or fell.

Whether this happened by night or day, we do not know—probably by night. That she lay for some time unconscious—for hours, maybe—is certain. Aroused by those who found her, she had no memory of what had occurred. At first they had thought her dead. When she stared at them dazed, they told her she had jumped. Soon she heard the Voice of Saint Catherine, bidding her to be of good cheer. The Voice said that she would be cured and that those at Compiègne would have succor. For several days she could neither eat nor drink but was comforted by Saint Catherine, who again assured her that Compiègne would be relieved before Saint Martin's winter day (November 11). Then presently she was able to eat and was soon cured. Compiègne was in fact relieved through the efforts of her two old comrades, Poton Saintrailles and the Count of Vendôme, October 25.

As soon as Joan was able to travel, arrangements were made to deliver her to the English.

The people filled the streets to see her pass

It was about mid-November that the Maid, strongly guarded and in chains, set out on that dreary journey across Flanders which would have its end in Rouen. What was the manner of her parting from the ladies of Beaurevoir whose lord, for a price, was sending her to her doom! What could they say to her?

By way of Cambrai, Arras and St.-Riquier, the Maid and her armored guards rode toward the sea. The people of the towns and villages filled the streets to see her pass and many prayed openly, for they believed her sent from God. At Arras, where the cavalcade paused for a day or more, some friendly soul secretly gave her files with which to escape from prison. They were found and taken from her.

Beyond St.-Riquier was the castle of Drugy, where in a little tower she passed the night. At Drugy churchmen and citizens from the town came to see her, showing much pity, for they regarded her "as persecuted, being very innocent." Another day and they had reached Le Crotoy, with its square, gloomy castle overlooking the sea. Cheerless it must have been but better than riding in chains. Here for the present the journey ended.

Joan was supposedly being taken to Paris for trial and Le Crotoy was by no means on the way. One reason for taking this route was that most of the towns between Beaurevoir and Paris were in French hands. Another reason was that neither Bedford nor Cauchon wished to try her in Paris, which was none too well content with English rule. Rouen, safely English, was the spot they had chosen. Le Crotoy, therefore, was not so far off the road and being handy to England was a good, safe place to keep the prisoner while the Church was locating the trial. This took time; weeks dragged by—Joan meantime in her gloomy tower awaiting she knew not what. She was not entirely without company. That gallant knight Aimond de Macy had come with those who brought her from Beaurevoir. Also, there was a prisoner from Amiens, a chancellor of the Church, who often held services in the castle and heard Joan in confession. Once some ladies came from Abbéville, fifteen miles distant, to visit this "marvel of her sex," as they regarded her. They invoked blessings on her and she kissed them at parting, commending them to God, asking them to pray for her. Weeping, they left her.

Cauchon finally got his permission to try Joan at Rouen and lost no time in bringing her there. Sometime during the last half of December—it was near Christmas Day—the Maid, chained and under heavy guard, was put into a barge and, accompanied by many armed boats, conveyed from Le Crotoy across the mouth of the Somme, there very wide. At St.-Valéry on the other side she was received by a large body of Burgundian soldiers. That day they traveled twenty miles down the wintry coast, lodging at night in the castle of Eu. Next day they passed through Dieppe to the great castle of Arques-la-Bataille, where again she found shelter. One shudders to think of that bitter winter journey, racking days in chains with only dungeons at night; one pictures the open-mouthed, staring crowds of Eu, of Dieppe, the helpless sympathy in the poor villages as the troopers clanked through the streets, in their midst a girl not yet nineteen, the Maid of miracles, going to her doom.

One more day, this time through Norman hamlets, then nightfall, and heights above a far-lying river, Joan and her guards looking down through the dim light on a collection of towers and spires and huddled houses—Rouen. A little more and they have passed down the steep descent to the city, crossed a drawbridge, entered a castle yard and heard the great portcullis clang down behind them. Rough, brief formalities, after which the Maid of France is led to a dungeon in one of the castle towers and delivered to ribald English guards. It is an even two years, perhaps to the very day, since with Durand Laxart she left Domrémy, directed by angel Voices, to reclaim France.

XIX

ROUEN

Earl of Warwick, chief jailer

Joan was in Rouen nearly two months before she was brought to trial. Pierre Cauchon, Bishop of Beauvais, was making preparations for his *beau procès,* as he called it. He was picking just the right men as his assistants and he was gathering and manufacturing evidence that he believed would not only convict the Maid but likewise convince the public of her guilt as a heretic, a blasphemer and a witch. To convince the public was important, for if he was to hold the great office of Archbishop of Rouen he must be in favor with the people of that city and its tributary towns.

The bishop began by sending special agents to Domrémy and Greux to collect evidence of Joan's early life that could be used against her. He wanted to prove that even in childhood she had practiced spells and other witchwork. The venture did not turn out well; the agents only brought back reports that Joan had been much beloved in Domrémy, where she had done nothing worse than sing and dance with other children under a so-called "Fairy Tree," sometimes hanging wreaths on it. One of those sent declared he had learned nothing about her that he would not gladly have heard of his own sister. Cauchon called him a traitor and at first refused to pay the cost of the inquiry. The reports about the Fairy Tree, however, suggested witchcraft and might be twisted into something damaging to the Maid.

Cauchon had other troubles. Some of the priests summoned to assist him did not like the prospect and even criticized his methods. Furious, the bishop denounced these objectors, so fiercely threatening to drown them that a number of them fled the country. One of them, a worthy man named Nicolas de Houppeville, was thrown into prison and only saved from exile or worse through the interference of powerful friends. It was Cauchon's claim that he was prosecuting Joan for the good of her soul, but De Houppeville, later testifying, said: "I have never thought that the Bishop of Beauvais engaged in this trial for the good of the faith and through zeal for justice, with the desire to redeem Joan. He simply obeyed the hate he had conceived for her because of her devotion to the party of the King of France and merely followed his own inclinations. I saw this when he rendered an account to the regent of his negotiations for the purchase of Joan, being unable to contain himself for joy." Many others near Cauchon during this period expressed the same opinion, among them the notary and recorder, G. Manchon, of unquestioned integrity.

Joan's situation during these long weeks can hardly be imagined. As prisoner of the Church she was entitled to decent lodging with female attendance. Neither was allowed her. She was confined in a tower "near the fields" of the great castle of Philip Augustus and her chief jailer was the Earl of Warwick. Warwick has been called "the father of courtesy" but because Joan was charged with being a heretic and a witch, "courtesy" required no more than that she be kept alive until the day of execution.

Her tower dungeon, being but a little above the ground ("eight steps" by one witness), was sunless, for the walls were thick, the windows mere slits. She was not free to walk about; her hands and feet were heavily chained. Connecting them, another chain ran round her body and was locked to a great block of wood. She carried this load of chains by day and at night slept in them. They were never removed—she was a witch; without them she might fly away.

Her dungeon was unclean and bitterly cold. She had no privacy of any sort. By day and by night four or five English guards were in her cell, drunken rioters of brutal behavior and evil language. Notary Manchon spoke of them as "miserable men"— mere tramps who sang and rioted and buffeted her about, taunting her with her fate. At one moment they pretended that she was about to be released; the next, they shouted at her that she would be tortured and burned.

In such a place how did she keep from going mad? Her Voices helped but because of the noise in her cell she could not always hear them. Time and again she begged Warwick to transfer her to the Church prisons, a prayer that was never granted. That after seven weeks of such torture she was still able to go before her judges and answer as she did must be held the crowning miracle of her miraculous life.

She had visitors: privileged persons who came out of curiosity, to stare and ask questions or to taunt and revile her. Warwick one day brought a little group, among them one who must indeed have been callous to face her, John of Luxemburg. With him was that friendly knight, Aimond de Macy, whom the Maid was glad enough to see. It was De Macy who told of this visit.

Addressing the Maid, John of Luxemburg said to her: "Joan, I have come to buy you back; on condition, however, that you promise never again to arm yourself against us." The poor prisoner regarded him scornfully.

"In God's name," she said, "you mock me; for I know well that you have neither the power nor the wish."

On John's insisting, she answered: "I know well that these English will put me to death, believing after my death to gain the kingdom of France. But if there were a hundred thousand *godons* more than now they would not have the kingdom."

An English lord, the Earl of Stafford, drew his dagger halfway from its sheath, to strike the prisoner. Warwick prevented him. Joan must not be allowed so merciful a death.

It may very well have happened that the little King of England was one of Joan's visitors—that she saw him, as her Voices had foretold. The little King was in Rouen when Joan was brought there and remained there for several months. His residence was in the great castle where she was held prisoner; the Earl of Warwick, governor of the castle, being at the same time guardian of the little King and jailer of the Maid. The royal boy would surely wish, even demand, to see the witch of whom he must often have heard. Such a visit would be very private and the knowledge of it kept secret.

The Maid had good reason for her statement that she knew the English meant to put her to death. Not only had they often declared they would do this but news had come to her that a woman whom she had known as Pierronne, a convert of Brother Richard, had been burned in Paris for claiming to have visions and even more for declaring that the works of Joan had been done by the will of God. If poor, harmless Pierronne had been thus brought to the stake, how much more fiercely would the English demand the ashes of one who had destroyed their armies and crowned the rival King. Heretic and witch she was to them, and a deadly enemy. Abandoned by the King she had crowned, the city she had redeemed, the captains she had led, what hope had she who such a little while before had been the idol of France?

Sixty against one

For the trial of Joan of Arc, Cauchon managed to get together a full sixty men of the Church, among them the best and certainly the wariest minds in France. Besides this great array there were some twenty or thirty others who by invitation appeared at the *beau procès* from time to time as special advisers, or merely to look on and admire. This was the prosecution. Ranged against it the defense made a poor showing, for it consisted of but a single person, a peasant girl of nineteen with neither advocate nor counsel.

Not all of Cauchon's assistants were moved by malignity and hatred of the Maid. Many, it is true, were tarred by the same brush as himself, men hating what England hated and in deadly fear of Bedford. Others served for the few frances it would put into their lean purses; still others were sincere—religious zealots who believed the accused guilty as charged—while among the sixty were a few with little taste for the bishop's undertaking—kindly men who grew to believe in the Maid and would have saved her if they could.

Two of the assistants, Prosecutor Jean d'Estivet and Nicolas Loiseleur, a canon of Rouen, were neither more nor less than prison spies, thoroughly vicious and detestable. On the other hand the recorders of the testimony, Manchon, Boisguillaume and Taquel, were for their time liberal, fair-minded men, certainly far better than those about them. Well for us that this is so; otherwise the story of the Maid would have been worse than lost for it would have been blackened and distorted out of all semblance.

It was on the morning of February 21, 1431, that Cauchon's grand tribunal finally assembled in the Chapel Royal of the great castle and Joan was brought before it. Two years earlier lacking two days, she had ridden from the western gate of the castle of

Vaucouleurs and Robert de Baudricourt had called: "Go, and let come what may!"

Whatever that grim soldier had imagined he had never pictured this present scene: fifty or more stern, shaven, black-gowned men facing a single figure on a bench, Joan in a page's suit, also of black, the face above it white with prison pallor, her hands chained. Around and about pressed the crowd, as many as could get in the place.

The bailiff who conducted her to and from the prison said later that in the beginning Joan asked to have counsel, saying she was too inexperienced to hold her own. She was told that she would have no counsel—that she must reply of herself as best she could. Further, she was warned that to clear her conscience she must answer truthfully the questions they would ask her; she was commanded to lay her hands on the Bible and make oaths to do this. Joan here made her first recorded answer; she said: "I do not know upon what you wish to question me. There may be things you will ask me that I must not tell you."

"Will you swear to tell the truth concerning the questions that will be asked of you as to the faith and what you know?"

"As to my father and mother and what I have done since I came to France, I will swear willingly. But as to the revelations from God I have never told them or revealed them to anyone except King Charles and no more would I reveal them here, even should you cut off my head. For I had them through visions and from my secret Council, to reveal to nobody."

At this defiant answer the court broke into confusion. The prisoner had refused to reveal her visions. The bishop and a half dozen or more of his assistants began shouting at the Maid and at each other, the witness being interrupted at every word she tried to speak. Two special secretaries employed by Bedford were excitedly putting down whatever they could catch that would be against her; the regular recorders could get nothing of value. Manchon shouted that unless order was maintained he

would not accept the responsibility of making a record at all. The Maid waited while the battle raged around her. Quiet at length restored, and again urged to take the oath, she finally knelt, her hands on the missal, and swore to speak the truth, but in a way that would omit her visions.

In answer now to questions, she gave her name, birthplace, age as nearly as she knew it, adding that her religious teaching had been from her mother. She refused, however, to say the Lord's Prayer until she was heard in confession, which had been denied her. Later she asked that she be transferred to the Church prisons. This too was denied and she was threatened with certain conviction if she attempted to escape. She looked wearily at her chains and begged to be relieved of them. But they answered that she had more than once tried to escape, for which reason the order had been given to put her in chains. She said: "It is true I have wished to escape, and would still do so. It is the privilege of every prisoner to escape if he can."

The first session was a brief one. That evening at Cauchon's home Manchon's record of the day was compared with that made by the English secretaries and the recorder was sharply reprimanded because his notes differed from theirs. Of this Manchon said later: "Many times in writing the process I had to undergo reprimands from the Bishop of Beauvais and divers other doctors. They wished to force me to write according to their imagination and contrary to what Joan had meant to say. They told me in Latin to employ other terms in such fashion as to change the sense of the word, and to record other things than those I heard. But I never wrote except according to my hearing and my conscience."

Manchon may not have won in every contest with the judges but many of those present later bore witness to his courage. Had he not been a person of great ability, with influence in Rouen, Cauchon would hardly have let him continue the work.

"At the age of thirteen I heard a Voice"

It was through Manchon's complaint that the scene of the trial was next day transferred from the Royal Chapel to the State Chamber, a room from which the crowds were excluded. English guards were placed at the door and only a select audience admitted.

On this morning Joan again refused to take the oath to reply to all that might be asked of her, saying more than once: "I took the oath yesterday; that certainly should be enough."

She finally swore to speak truly on matters touching the faith. She said: "If you were well informed concerning me you would wish that I might be well out of your hands."

Asked if she had learned some special work in youth, she said: "Yes, to sew linen and to spin and in these things I fear no woman in Rouen."

When they asked her something to which she did not wish to reply she merely said: *"Passez outre"* (that is, "Pass to something else").

On this day, of her own will, she told of her Voices and of her start from Vaucouleurs.

"At the age of thirteen I had a Voice from God to aid and direct me," she began. "The first time it caused me great fear."

The courtroom became silent; the judges leaned forward to listen.

"The Voice came about the hour of noon, in my father's garden. I had not fasted the day before. I heard this Voice at the right, on the side toward the church, and rarely it came without light. This light came from the same side as the Voice and there was ordinarily a great light. . . . If I was in a wood the Voice came to me. It seemed to me a worthy Voice and I believe it was sent to me on the part of God. After having heard it three times I recognized it as the Voice of an angel. This Voice has always guarded me and I know it well."

Continuing, she said the angel had taught her good conduct and told her she must go to France. She had answered that she was a poor girl, knowing neither how to ride nor conduct war.

We get the impression of a quiet courtroom with Joan telling her story about in her own way. Here and there she was asked a brief question but for the most part she was not interrupted. When she reached the point of her meeting with the King, they stopped her. They wished to know by what signs she recognized him.

"*Passez outre,*" she said, and again: "Spare me; *passez outre.*"

But Joan's hardships had told on her and on this second day we get the first hint of an illusion as to this sign, an aberration that would develop a sad fantasy as the days passed and her sufferings of mind and body increased. On this occasion she went no further than to say that "several others *heard* and *saw* the Voice that came to her," but later she would say much more and her prosecutors would not fail to play upon this weakness. On all other matters her mind was and to the end remained sound and clear. A moment later she was telling simply enough of her attack on Paris.

Joan's trial and her story became the great interest of Rouen. On the third morning a full court was present, Cauchon and sixty assistant judges. Joan again refusing to take a general oath, there followed a long dispute in the course of which she warned Cauchon that he assumed a great burden in claiming to be her judge. She finally swore to answer truly concerning whatever related to her indictment. Questioned as to when and how her Voice still came to her, she said it had come yesterday in her prison and again today. It had awakened her and when she had asked for counsel, the Voice had told her to reply boldly to her questioners and that God would comfort her. Here again she warned Cauchon: "You say that you are my judge. Consider well what you do, for in truth I am sent from God and you place yourself in great danger."

Advice like that, from one whose warnings had been followed

by results, could not fail to send a shiver through the superstitious Cauchon. He did not pursue the subject then but at a later time asked her what she had meant by it. She only repeated that he put himself in great danger, adding, "And I warn you of it in order that if our Lord chastises you I have done my duty in telling you."

The Bishop uneasily asked her what the danger was. She did not answer, but her warning, as we shall see, was not an empty one.

The tedious questioning went on. In every way they tried to trap her. Some of the judges themselves declared that questions were asked that the most skilled and learned doctor would not have known how to answer. Yet she replied calmly, wisely and with a presence of mind that amazed them. She appears never to have lost her temper though her judges constantly lost theirs.

It was on the third day that she made an answer that seems nothing less than inspired. Suddenly out of a clear sky she was asked: "Do you know yourself to be in the grace of God?"

That is to say, in a state of grace. The judges leaned forward. One of them exclaimed: "It is a mighty question: she is not obliged to answer!" Cauchon turned on him fiercely: "You would have done better to be silent!"

It was indeed a mighty question. Whichever way she answered could count against her. Joan herself realized this; then quietly, without a wasted word, replied: "If I am not, God put me there; if I am, God keep me there"; and in the silence that followed added: "I would be the most sorrowful in all the world to know myself not in the grace of God."

Said one of the notaries later: "Before these words the examiners were stupefied." They left the matter there and asked her of her childhood. She told of the battles between the boys of Domrémy and those of Maxey, of her own warm zeal that her King should regain his kingdom. Asked of the Fairy Tree, she spoke of her childhood games beneath it and of the fairies having been seen, as she had heard, by her godmother.

"Sometimes I went there to play with the other girls and made under the Tree wreaths of flowers for the picture of Our Lady of Domrémy. . . . I have seen little girls hang wreaths on the branches of the Tree and have sometimes done this with the others. Sometimes we brought them away; sometimes left them there."

She said that when she had known that she must come to France she had taken little part in their play—as little as she could. Whether since the age of understanding she had danced around the Tree she did not know; but at times she may well have danced there with the others, though she had sung more than she had danced.

Her judges listened greedily, for they meant to twist this innocent testimony into a confession of witchwork, black magic that would bring her to the stake. Today it is hard for us to realize that only a few hundred years ago, in a world of real men and women and sunlight, so evil a thing as this could have been true. That it *is* true we know, for the record of it all was made by her enemies themselves.

"Dress is of small things the least"

We have seen something of the misery of Joan's prison, a hideous place in which she could find no moment of privacy even for prayer. In that bedlam how she must have yearned for the quiet retirement of a church, the consolation of an altar. The castle of Philip Augustus was a huge affair, with its own chapel located in the court through which the Maid each day must pass on the way to her examination. Of Bailiff Massieu, who conducted her, she begged to be allowed to pause before this chapel. She did not ask to enter but only to kneel at the entrance and pray. Massieu, a kindly man, consented willingly enough and Joan, bowed to the ground, devotedly said her prayers. Word of this coming to Cauchon and to prosecutor

D'Estivet, they forbade it, the latter fiercely threatening Massieu with prison. When Massieu repeated the offense D'Estivet in person stood before the chapel and prevented the prayer.

On the fourth day of her trial Joan was asked if she had seen Saint Michael and the others as in flesh; she answered. "I saw them with the eyes of my body as well as I see you yourself and when they went away from me I wept and greatly wished they had taken me with them."

Often she declared that her Voices told her to "answer boldly" and sometimes she said that to certain questions her Voices had not given her permission to reply. Again she was not sure as to what the Voices had told her, owing to the noise made by her ruffian guards. Of her coming to France she said: "I would rather have been drawn and quartered than to have come to France without the permission of God."

For a woman to wear male dress was against the old Biblical law. Hoping to convict her of having taken it of her own will or by the order of some captain, they brought up this point time and again. Once she said to them: "Dress is of small things the least," and added: "I have not taken this dress by the advice of anyone whomsoever; I have not taken this dress nor done any other thing except by the command of God and His angels."

"Do you think the commandment given you to dress as a man is lawful?"

"All that I have done has been by the commandment of God; if He had ordered me to take another I would have taken it, since it would have been by the commandment of God."

"Did you take it by the order of Robert de Baudricourt?"

They were trying to wear her down, to exasperate her; she answered simply: "No."

Again and again in different forms they repeated their questions, in the end to get no more than the quiet statement: "I have done nothing except by the commandment of God."

Of her revelation to the King she would utter no word though they tried with all their skill to wring from her these secrets. She freely spoke of the sword that had been brought by her request from Fierbois, and of the banner that had been made for her at Tours. Of the banner she said: "I had a standard, the field of which was sown with lilies. There, also, was the image of God holding the world and two angels at His sides. It was white in color, of linen or fustian. There was inscribed on it these names, 'JESUS MARIA,' as it seems to me, and it was fringed with silk."

This description recorded by her enemies is nothing less than poetry. Joan's words were often of that simple grandeur and loveliness.

They tried to upset her with confusing questions about the banner and the sword. Which had she loved the more? was one of their futile queries. The banner, she told them, far more, "forty times more"; and her gentle reason: "I carried the banner myself, to avoid killing anybody; I have never killed a man."

Yet she could be relentless in her cause. Once asked if she had ever been in a place where English were killed, she replied sharply: "In God's name, of course! How softly you speak! Why did they not leave France and go back to their own country?"

At this an English lord present spoke admiringly of her. "If only she were English!" he said.

The Maid's answers were caught up and repeated by the people of Rouen, who began to declare openly that she was being evilly treated. Even some of the judges were moved in her favor. They whispered among themselves that she should be taken from her wretched dungeon to the less disgraceful Church prison. "Many were of this opinion but none dared to speak," one of them testified. Cauchon, dominated by Bedford and War-wick, could not in any case have made the change, but nowhere is there a hint that he was so inclined.

Long, weary days of examination went by, Joan holding her own against the great array of doctors. Harassed by day, beset by a hundred horrors at night, never alone, never free from the galling chains, how did she do it? "The doctors themselves went out of there very fatigued"—the testimony of one of them. And these were men, each morning rested and refreshed. But perhaps unlike Joan they did not have the support and the comfort of angels.

She spoke fearless of consequence. At most they could only destroy her body. Sometimes she prophesied; as for instance, one day: "Before seven years the English will lose a greater prize than they did before Orléans and they will lose everything in France."

They stormed at her but they could not change or move her. "I know it by revelation," she told them, "and before seven years it will happen."

They were disturbed and fearful. They tried to make her fix the date. She did not know that, she said, but wished that it might be soon. Saint Catherine and Saint Margaret had revealed to her only the fact. The "greater prize," as we now know, was Paris, which did yield within the seven years of her prophecy. Joan made no definite predictions that were not fulfilled. She was only uncertain as to the time of occurrence.

They tried to confuse her with silly questions concerning the dress, ornaments and features of the saints. What promises had they ever made her? She refused to answer; whereupon a tumult broke out, in the midst of which she said the saints had promised that the King would be restored and that they would conduct her to paradise. There was another promise but of that she would not speak. Before three months she would tell them. They took this to mean that she expected to be delivered from prison in that time. This may have been her meaning, for when they were insistent she said: "Ask me again in three months; then I will answer. This I know well: that my King will regain the kingdom of France. I know it as well as I know you are here before me as judges. I should be dead if it were not for the revelation that comforts me each day."

Later they asked her: "Was Saint Michael without dress?"

"Do you think the Lord had nothing with which to clothe him?"

"Did he have hair?"

"Why should it have been cut off?"

Questions like these were flung at her from every side, sometimes two or three at once. Bailiff Massieu later testified: "Before she replied to one question someone interrupted to ask a new one, which tended to upset her answers. Several times she said to them: 'Fair lords, speak one after the other.'"

Now and then during the rapid fire some one of the assistants braver than the others objected that such procedure was not just. One of these said: "It is not necessary to proceed thus; you break our ears."

Cauchon shouted: "Silence, and let the judges speak!" To which the other answered: "It is necessary, however, that I acquit my conscience."

Tumult followed. The offender was ordered from the court and told not to return until he was sent for.

"Joan, you speak well!"

Regularly each morning before the questioning began, Joan was commanded to make oath to reply to all questions and each morning, as in the beginning, she refused, being finally allowed to take the oath in her own way. On the sixth day of examination but forty of the assistants were present. The *beau procès* was losing the sympathy of the examiners. Those who dared to remain away sent excuses. During this day Joan was asked: "Did you not say that pennons made like yours would be lucky?"

"What I did say was: 'Enter boldly among the English,' and I did this myself."

"Did you say to them that if they carried them boldly they would have luck?"

"I told them plainly what would happen, and what will still happen."

At another time they asked: "Do you know that those of your party have offered service, mass and prayer for you?"

"I know nothing of that. If they have done so it has not been by my order; and if they have prayed for me I believe they have done no wrong."

"Did those of your party believe firmly that you were sent from God?"

"I do not know if they believed it. I leave that to their conscience. But whether they believe it or not, still I am sent from God."

"Do you not think that if they believe you were sent by God they have a good belief?"

"If they believe I was sent by God, they are not deceived."

Wishing to convict her of accepting worship, they asked her if she did not well know the sentiments of those who had kissed her hands and feet and clothing. To this she replied that many were glad to see her, and kissed her hands and her clothing, but no more than she could help.

"The poor came to me gladly," she said, "for the reason that I did not cause them unhappiness but uplifted them as much as was in my power."

Answers like these circulating through Rouen could not improve the public's opinion of Cauchon's case. Once even one of the judges called out: "Joan, you speak well!"

She told them the story of her leap from the tower at Beaurevoir. When she had finished, they asked: "Did you not say you would rather die than be in the hands of the English?"

Joan regarded the chains that were eating into her flesh, and thought of her fearful prison. Then she said: "I would rather give my soul to God than be in the hands of the English."

A distinguished Norman lawyer, named Lohier, came to Rouen. Cauchon sent for him and asked his opinion of the case against Joan. Lohier frankly replied that it was not legal for several reasons: one being that Joan had no counsel; another, that it was carried on behind closed doors; a third, that no wit-

nesses were summoned from the other side. Cauchon fell into
a great fury, declaring he would continue as begun. He told
Lohier to remain and hear more of the trial. But Lohier had
heard enough and the same day left Rouen.

Lohier's protest had an immediate effect: Cauchon continued
his *beau procès*, but not "as begun." Too many of his assistants
were beginning to think like Lohier. The bishop stopped all examinations for a week; when they were resumed they were no
longer held in the fine State Chamber before sixty or more distinguished churchmen but in the dim and fetid seclusion of
Joan's prison with an attendance of no more than six or seven,
including bailiff and notaries. The *beau procès* had shrunken to
a shabby affair—shabby and shameful, for the Maid's answers
could no longer reach the people outside; she no longer had even
a glimpse of blue sky and sunshine that she got crossing the court
nor the change of scene thus afforded. In her chains she sat on
her bed, the half dozen black-robed men, on benches and stools,
grouped about her. The light was dim, the notaries needed
candles. She was no longer required to swear.

They asked her of Compiègne. She told them wearily of her
capture—of her warning at Melun and of the fatal sortie at
Margny.

"Were you not told after Melun that you would be taken?"

"Yes, several times; so to speak, every day. I asked of my
Voices that when I was taken I might die soon without long
suffering in prison. They told me that I must accept all in good
will and that this must be; but they did not tell me the time."

She told them that the sortie on Margny had not been made
by the order of her Voices. Continuing, she gave the story of her
capture, closing: "The river was between Compiègne and the
place where I was taken. And there was only between Compiègne and the place where I was taken just the river, the *boulevard* and the moat of the said *boulevard*."

Since her first curious statement as to the sign and secret between her and the King, when she had declared that several there

had *heard* and *seen* the Voice, her inquisitors had for some reason avoided this subject. They now came back to it and while on all other matters the Maid's mind remained clear, there can be no doubt that on this subject she had developed an illusion. Among other things she told them that after the King had seen the sign the angel had brought, she, Joan, had gone to a near-by chapel and later had heard that after her departure more than three hundred persons had seen the sign.

Again brought to this subject, she said that the sign had been delivered to the archbishop by the angel, that it was a crown of the richest sort and that the angel who brought it came from on high; also that she in his company had ascended the steps of the King's audience chamber, the angel first, then Joan, who said to the King: "Sire, behold your sign; and receive it." Other angels, she said, had accompanied them.

"Of those who were in the company of the angel, were all of the same form?"

"Some resembled each other and some not, as I saw them. Some of them had wings; also, some had crowns, others not, and in the company were Saint Catherine and Saint Margaret. They were with the angel mentioned, and the other angels also, as far as within the King's audience chamber."

Joan had walked with the invisible. What memory of it remained in her poor, disturbed brain we shall never know. Her story, a sad mixture of allegory and illusion, became more fantastic with each telling. She confused her meeting with the King at Chinon with the coronation and was no longer clear as to the hour or the time of year. Some writers have thought that the Maid was trifling with her judges. Such a conclusion is unworthy. Joan was not in a position to trifle and in her right mind would have been the last person to invent such a tale. First, because her habit was truth; second, because her good sense would tell her that it was exactly such a contradictory tale of signs and wonders that would bring her to the stake. Joan's long privation and mental anguish had upset her mind on this one theme. Many persons, otherwise quite sane, are subject to such special illusions. Joan was absolutely clear on everything except this matter of the sign. Immediately following her story of the angel, she was asked. "Why did he come to you rather than to another?"

And she returned this beautiful answer: "It pleased God thus through a simple Maid to drive out the adversaries of the King."

In the beginning Joan's examinations had ended at noon, holding her on the rack during a stretch of four hours. Cauchon decided that this was not enough and another session was held in the afternoon. This was to wear her down, to drive her into fatal admissions. The strongest witness will often give way after a few days or even hours of cross-examination. Again and again we ask ourselves: How did this young girl manage to hold her own through those weeks of torture? And then we come to a passage like the following and find her clinging to her faith in God and men; likewise to her Voices! Of her own accord, answering no question, one day she said: "Saint Catherine has told me that I will have succor. I do not know if it will be delivery from prison or if when I shall be in judgment [brought to execution] some trouble may arise through which I shall be delivered. I think it will be one way or the other. Oftener my Voices say to me that I shall be delivered through great victory and afterward have told me: 'Take all in good part; have no care for your martyrdom; from it you will come finally to the kingdom of paradise.' This my Voices say to me simply and clearly and without fail. And I call the martyrdom the sorrow and adversity that I suffer in prison. I do not know whether I shall have to suffer a greater one but leave that to our Lord."

In all the proceedings there is no passage more pathetic than this.

"After this revelation, do you believe that you can commit mortal sin?"

"I know nothing of that, but in all refer myself to God."

At another time they asked: "Has the angel not failed you in allowing you to be captured?"

"Since it was pleasing to our Lord, I believe it was for the best that I was taken."

"In the gifts of grace, has not the angel failed you?"

"How has it failed me when it comforts me every day?"

Now and again the question of Joan's dress came up. Once they said to her: "Since you have asked to hear mass, does it not seem to you that it would be more honest to hear it in woman's dress?"

She agreed to take woman's dress in which to hear mass but said that upon her return she would take again the habit she wore. She could not wear any other, she told them, in the prison among her guards. Oh, that hideous prison! The thought of it becomes more sickening as we read. The horrors of it cannot be put into words.

They asked her if she would submit her acts and deeds to the judgment of the Church. To Joan, the Church was represented by the men before her—her enemies. She answered that all her words and deeds were in the hands of God—that she had no wish to do or say anything opposed to the Christian faith.

"Will you submit to the laws of the Church?" they asked.

Joan knew little of Church law and science but she felt that this was likely to be a serious matter. She would tell them, she said, on Saturday; meaning she would consult her Voices; also perhaps the spy Loiseleur, of whom we shall presently hear more.

They asked her if she did nothing without the permission of her Voices. She replied that they had been fully answered as to that—that if they looked in their record they would find it. Some of those present later testified that often she replied like this and that when the record was consulted they found that in each case it was as she said.

Again, as often before, they asked her of Saint Michael: how she knew him; how she could be certain he was not an evil spirit. She had known these things, she said, by his manner of speech and his good teachings.

"What doctrine did he teach you?"

"He told me to be a good child in all things and that God would help me and among other things that I would go to the rescue of the King. And the greater part of what the angel taught me is in this record. And the angel spoke to me of *the pity that was of the kingdom of France.*"

"*The pity that was of the kingdom of France!*" Who but Joan could have found that sublime phrase?

Loiseleur

The episode of Nicolas Loiseleur was probably the most detestable feature of Cauchon's *beau procès*. It was the custom of the Inquisition in dealing with suspected heretics to place near the accused a spy, to give false advice and through pretense of friendship to obtain damaging evidence. Loiseleur, a canon of Rouen, was selected for this work in Joan's case, assisted by the prosecutor, D'Estivet, both favorites of Cauchon and as villainous a pair of scoundrels as ever disguised themselves in holy garb. Loiseleur, pretending to be a shoemaker from Joan's country and like herself a prisoner, was from time to time allowed to enter her tower and speak with her privately. A number of those connected with the trial later told of this. Notary Manchon, a man of honesty and good will, was in a position to give the fullest account. Manchon testified that Cauchon, Warwick and Loiseleur said to him and his associate:

"This Joan tells marvels of her apparitions. To know more fully the truth from her mouth we have reached this conclusion. Master Nicolas will pretend he is from Lorraine and of Joan's party; he will enter the prison in short habit [citizen dress] and the guards will retire and leave them alone."

There was to the adjoining room an opening made expressly [probably a stone removed from the partition], where we were placed, my associate and myself, to hear what Joan

would say. We were there hearing all without being seen.
Loiseleur entered into conversation with Joan and gave her
news, imagined according to his fancy. After having spoken
of her King, he spoke of her revelations. Joan replied to his
questions, persuaded that he was of her country and her party.
The bishop and Warwick told us to record the replies made
by Joan. I answered that this should not be done, that it was
not honest to use such means.

Loiseleur, however, continued his visits to Joan, bringing
whatever she told him to Cauchon, who used it in preparing
the questions he would ask her. Furthermore, he went to her
at night in his real character of priest, robed and hooded, his
voice somehow disguised. He had been sent to confess her, he
said, and the poor, beset girl, hungry for the consolation of confession, may have given him her confidence. Manchon said that
in general the Maid was never led before the judges without
having conferred with Loiseleur.

Accepting Manchon's statement as fact, all this must have
happened well along in the trial when Joan's mind was less keen.
She could hardly have been so continuously deceived in the beginning and one may ask why she was not warned by her Voices.
That Loiseleur played the double role of priest and prisoner is
borne out by other witnesses. But perhaps Joan was not altogether deceived. There is little trace of his false advice in her
answers. Away from the matter of the sign, her mind is a con-
stant amazement. In the midst of treachery and torment she
may yet have known more than the testimony of these witnesses would lead us to believe.

*"It had borne the burden, it had
earned the honor"*

It is the last day of Joan's regular examination.
On this day seven priests assemble in her dim cell with the
usual notaries. Cauchon is present, also the Vice Inquisitor of
Rouen, who serves unwillingly, and Jean de Lafontaine, a re-
spectable man appointed by Cauchon as examiner to give his
case a better appearance. Among the others are Isambard de la
Pierre, a friendly but timid soul dominated by Cauchon and
Warwick.

This last day was to be memorable though it began with one
of the usual questions as to the form and apparel of Saint Michael.
Joan answered: "He was in the form of a wise and upright man.
Of the dress and other things I will say nothing further." And
presently she added: "I believe as firmly in the words and deeds
of Saint Michael who appeared to me as I believe that our Lord
suffered passion and death for us; and what moves me to believe
this, is the good advice, comfort and doctrine he has brought
and given me."

Then again they asked her if she would submit all her words
and deeds, whether of good or evil, to the determination of the
Church; that is, accept its judgment. Joan may or may not have
taken advice on this subject. At all events she knew that if she
submitted to the Church in the person of the men she saw before
her, her enemies, they could judge her guilty of witchcraft and
other offenses. Also, if she refused to submit, she could be held
guilty of heresy. In either case she could be burned. Without
reference to consequences she answered: "As for the Church,
I love it and wish to support it with all my power, for our
Christian faith. It is not I that should be prevented from going
to church and hearing mass. As to the good works I have done
and my coming to France, I would leave that to God who sent
me to Charles, King of France."

"Will you refer your words and acts to the judgment of the Church?"

"I refer them to God who sent me, to our Lady and to all the blessed saints of paradise. And I think it is all one, our Lord and the Church, and that in this difficulties should not be made for me. Why do you make difficulty when it is all one?"

This heartfelt question meant nothing to these doctors of "celestial science." One of them, Pierre Maurice, explained to her that there was the Church of Heaven, called the Church Triumphant; also the Church on earth, called the Church Militant, consisting of the Pope, the priesthood and all good Christians. It was to the Church Militant that she was asked to submit. Much of this was new to Joan, something to be considered. She answered that she had been sent to the King by God and by the Church on high, to which Church she would submit all that she had done or would do. As to submitting to the Church Militant, she could not at present reply.

They left the matter for the time and asked what she had to say of the dress offered her in which to attend mass. She would not take it, she said, as yet, but if she should be condemned and led to execution she asked that they grant her request for a long garment and for her head a kerchief. She added: "For I would rather die than revoke what our Lord has made me do; and I firmly believe that our Lord will never let me be brought so low and that I soon may be rescued and by a miracle."

It was a belief that she would cherish almost to her last hour, a part of her unshaken faith. Farther along they asked: "Does God hate the English?"

"Of the love or hate that God has for the English or what God will do with their souls, I know nothing; but I know they will be driven out of France, except those who will die here, and that God will send victory to the French against the English."

In the depths of misery, with death staring her in the face, she could still make them such an answer!

"What arms did you offer at St.-Denis?"

"I offered an entire suit of white armor and a sword that I won before Paris."

"Why did you offer it?"

"I offered it through devotion as the custom of soldiers when wounded. And because I was wounded before Paris I offered them to Saint Denis, whose name is the war cry of France."

"Did you do this that your arms might be worshiped?"

"No."

On that day, during the noon recess, Joan was visited by De Lafontaine, the examiner, the well-meaning Isambard and another kindly priest, Brother Martin Ladvenue, a little group of pitying souls who came with advice. She should submit to the Church, they told her, to the Pope and the Holy Council, especially as in the Council were as many of her party as of the others. Joan at this time was very willing to have her case laid before the Pope and before the Holy Council among which were priests of her own party. The result of this advice appeared during the afternoon.

First, however, her questioners touched upon her banner, in the use of which they scented witchcraft.

"Did you ask of them [the saints] that by virtue of this standard you should gain all the battles in which you fought, and that you might have victory?"

"They told me that I should take it boldly and that God would aid me."

"Which aided the more, you the standard or the standard you?"

"The victory, whether from the standard or from me, came wholly from our Lord."

"Was the hope of victory based upon your standard or yourself?"

"It was founded upon our Lord and not elsewhere."

They tried this question in different ways but the answer did not vary. It was hard to squeeze witchcraft out of such a reply.

They took another tack and asked her if she would not reply to certain questions more fully if she were before the Pope. She answered that she had replied as truthfully as she knew. On a second mention of the Pope, she remembered what had been said by the priests who had visited her; Isambard, as it appears, gave her a signal.

"*Take* me to the Pope," she said, "and I will reply before him to all that I should."

It was a demand that Joan had a right to make but it fell like a bombshell in the midst of Cauchon's faithful, no less than four of whom were present. A tumult followed. The bishop asked fiercely who had been talking to the prisoner. He was told by the guard of the visit of De Lafontaine and the others during the noon hour, on which he savagely denounced them.

In the midst of all this Joan called out that since some of her own party were there she would submit to the Holy Council. Isambard, betrayed by his feelings, evidently upheld her, for Cauchon shouted at him: "Silence, in the devil's name!"

"Shall I register the submission?" asked Manchon.

"No!" snapped Cauchon, "and you will take good care not to write it!"

"Ha," said Joan, "you write well enough whatever is against me and will not write that which is for me."

The scene lasted a good while. The official record does not give it; it was reported by Manchon and others later. Warwick, who was present, threatened those who had visited Joan with drowning in the Seine; Isambard especially, for having signaled her. Quiet at last restored, Joan was asked about one of the rings she had worn—rings being well known to have magic power.

"Why did you like to look at this ring when you went into battle?"

"Out of pleasure and in honor of my father and my mother; and having this ring on my finger I have touched Saint Catherine who appeared to me. . . ."

"When the saints appeared to you did you not make them reverence by kneeling or inclining?"

"Yes, the most that I could I made to them, for I know that they are those who are of the kingdom of paradise."

"Do you know anything of those who go up into the air with fairies?"

"I have never done this or known of it, though I have often heard of it and that it happens on Thursday. I do not believe in it and I think it is sorcery."

On this last day Cauchon was determined to establish his charge of sorcery.

"Did not someone wave or turn your standard about the head of the King at his coronation?"

"Not that I know of."

"Why, rather than those of other captains, was it carried into the Church of Reims?"

It was their final question, and only Joan could have answered: "It had borne the burden; it had earned the honor."

In the old French: "*Il avoit esté à la paine, c'estoit bien raison que il fut à l'onneur*"—the words will live as long as the language.[1]

Joan's wearying days of cross-examination had come to an end. Cauchon did not like the turn of affairs and perhaps thought he had about all he would be likely to get from her. One against many, without counsel or advocate, under conditions indescribable, the Maid had more than held her own. After twelve days of inquisition such as no modern witness can ever know, she had ended with that serene and immortal answer. Many have testified of her wise and prudent replies to questions that would have puzzled the doctors themselves.

"In all conscience they asked her questions too difficult," said Brother Ladvenu; "they wished to catch her."

---

1. More literally, "It had been in the strife; it had good right to the honor." The rendering in the text is Mark Twain's and more closely conveys the subtle delicacy of the original, which is like an elusive perfume.

The Seventy Articles

It was on March 17 that Joan's examination ended. A week later a copy of the questions, with her answers to them, was brought to her prison and read to her. The official report says that she acknowledged its correctness and again asked that she might hear mass. On the next morning, which was Palm Sunday, the bishop and a few others came to her with the proposal that she take woman's dress. She asked that she might be permitted to hear mass in the dress she wore and further that she might receive the sacrament on Easter—to her a dear and precious privilege. Again asked if she would change her dress, she said: "You could very well allow me to hear mass in this dress and I desire it above anything. But change I cannot and it does not rest with me." And a little later she pleaded: "To wear it is nothing against the Church—and lays no burden upon my soul."

To Joan in her bleak desolation the consolation asked meant more than we can possibly imagine. It was denied.

Cauchon, meantime, had ordered a list of "articles" prepared from Joan's testimony—articles claiming to contain her "confessions" but which in reality were a mere mass of false charges, statements twisted out of all semblance to her words. They would be read to her and Cauchon offered to let her have one of the assistants to advise her as to her answers. She quietly thanked him for his interest in her welfare and added: "I have no intention to depart from the counsel of our Lord."

There were seventy of the articles and according to Cauchon they had been prepared with the aid of God, in the glory of the Lord and for the exaltation of the faith. In the first of them Joan was advised of the right and duty of her judges to prosecute and punish heretics and witches. Of this she said: "I well believe that our holy father, the Pope of Rome, and the bishops and others of the Church are to guard the Christian faith and to punish those who fall away from it; but as for myself as concerns my facts, I will submit only to the Church of Heaven; that is to say, to God, to the Virgin Mary and the saints of paradise. And I believe I have in no way failed in our Christian faith, nor would I fail in it. And I require . . ."

What it was that Joan required of them we shall never know, for the record of her answer breaks off here.

A few examples of the Seventy Articles will be enough to show their character. Following the charge of being a sorceress, witch, divineress, false prophetess, invoker of evil spirits and conjuress, a woman given to the practice of magic arts, a blasphemer of God and the saints, one given to inciting war and cruelly athirst for human blood, etc., etc., it was declared that even in childhood Joan had mixed and prepared the potions and spells of witchwork, made pacts with demons and evil spirits which she regularly consulted and had allowed herself to be adored and venerated.

Joan merely denied these things, adding that if she had been adored it had not been by her wish.

Other articles declared that at Domrémy fairies collected around the Tree and the spring and that the Maid—taught witchcraft by certain old women—had gone there at night to work evil spells.

Joan's only reply to this attempt to warp and twist the innocent play of childhood into something dark and loathsome was to refer to her former answers.

They charged that aided and abetted by demons she had hidden a sword at Fierbois in order that she might mislead her followers by finding it. Anyone else would indignantly have denied this accusation; Joan did no more than refer to her former answers.

When they piled up charges of heresy and blasphemy she listened patiently and replied that she was a good Christian, referring herself to God.

They charged her with placing her banner in the church at

Reims during the coronation, wishing in her pride and vain-glory to make others pay tribute to it.

"It had borne the burden; it had earned the honor!" They had twisted it into this. She referred them to that answer and to God.

The final article declared that before men worthy of the faith the Maid several times had confessed these charges to be true. Joan merely denied this, referring to her recorded answers.

The reading of the Seventy Articles consumed two long days. If Cauchon's purpose in them had been to goad his victim to violence and damaging confessions, it had failed. Weakened as Joan was, her health even then at the very breaking point, she had remained outwardly unmoved by the false charges, their wicked and cruel words.

A few days later the bishop and seven of his trusted assistants came again to her prison to hear her decision as to submitting her words and acts to the Church; that is, to themselves. Would she, they asked, abide by their verdict? Joan replied that her words and deeds proceeded from divine source. She would submit them only to the Lord, she said, "obeying always His good commandment."

"Are you not," they asked, "subject to the Church on earth, the Pope, the cardinals, the bishops and the rest?"

"I am, our Lord being first served."

"He intends that she shall die by law"

Joan next morning was taken desperately ill. The strain of long confinement and mental anguish had undermined her strength, upset her physical organism. She ate of a fish which Cauchon had sent her, it being Easter Sunday, and was seized with a violent congestion. It has been thought that the fish was poisoned but this is not likely. The bishop did not intend her to die in that way.

Three physicians were hastily sent for, two of whom testified

later. From them we learn that Joan, sick unto death as she
was, was still loaded with chains.[1] Warwick said to them: "I
have sent for you that you may try to cure her. The King [of
England—meaning Bedford] would not for anything in the world
have her die a natural death; for he holds her dear, having paid
dearly for her he intends she shall die by law and be burned.
Do therefore what is necessary. Attend her with great care,
and try to cure her."

The doctors advised bleeding. Warwick said: "A bloodlet-
ting? Take care! She is sly and could very well kill herself."

Nevertheless they bled the patient and she seemed better; then
D'Estivet came to the prison and standing over the sick girl
called her evil names and charged her with eating forbidden
food. Joan denied this but his insults threw her into a relapse.
Her fever returned and she was again at the point of death.
Warwick drove D'Estivet from the prison. D'Estivet was not
only Cauchon's prosecutor but a priest in high standing.

The Twelve Articles

Joan, hovering between life and death, was apparently untroubled by her persecutors for more than two weeks,
a period the details of which we shall never know. Cauchon did
not remain idle. Realizing that the Seventy Articles had not
advanced his case he had the number skillfully reduced to twelve,
omitting most of the distortions and false charges. The result
was a document as reasonable, under the circumstances, as could
be expected. Its substance may be briefly stated:

Joan claimed to have seen and spoken to the saints. They had
spoken to her at a profane place haunted by fairies.

She claimed to have been commanded by God to take the
dress of a man. She prophesied and still continued to prophesy.

She had left her home without consent and to the great grief
of her parents.

In company with an angel she claimed to have brought a

---

1. One of the notaries, Nicolas Taquel, also testified to this.

very precious crown and delivered it to the King as a sign.

She refused to submit her acts and words to the Church.

There was much more, but this was sufficient. Under the Church law of that day Joan could be convicted on her own words. The University of Paris, to which the articles would be submitted, could decide that her Voices were those of demons. In the matter of the sign she could be charged with falsehood and presumption. For prophesying she could be held guilty of devination and witchcraft. In refusing to submit to the Church she was open to the charge of heresy. As to her male dress, there was the authority of the Bible itself for holding it an abomination.

Cauchon's mistake had been in wanting a grand trial. With a few judges of his own kind he could have convicted Joan and sent her to the stake as promptly as poor Pierronne had been disposed of in Paris the year before. His idea had been to invite the admiration of Rouen, where he expected to become archbishop. Instead, he had stirred up the city in Joan's favor! As a result, his *beau procès* had shrunken from a great court in the State Chamber to a squalid hearing in a jail. Still, with Bedford and the English army behind him in one way or another he meant to win. From his assistants and others he invited opinions on the Twelve Articles. Nearly all agreed that Joan had committed the acts as charged and should be held guilty. Some who made this report were moved by cowardice. Others, ardent zealots, indorsed it in good faith. Still others, like Loiseleur, did so because they were mere human vermin eager to see this young girl put to death. The Twelve Articles were now sent to the University of Paris.

"I have said it all at my trial"

Joan's illness had begun on the first of April. On April 18, the bishop and seven of his assistants visited her "to console and recomfort her," as he said. She was to be admonished and exhorted to return to the "path of truth" and he offered "in all affection" to send someone to instruct her in order that she might know what to reply. We need only remember the "affection" that had invented the shameful Seventy Articles, to put a proper value on Cauchon's consolation and advice. Joan, weak and wasted as she was, still in death's shadow, was not deceived by it. She thanked them, however, and asked that in case of her death she be laid in consecrated ground.

She must submit to the Church, they told her, if she wanted the benefits of the Church. She replied wearily: "I would not know what further to say to you."

Exhausted as she was by her illness, they took turns in threatening and denouncing her as they had upon the witness stand. Once she said: "Let happen to me what must. I can do or say nothing further. I have said it all at my trial."

"You are no more than a pagan and a publican," they flung at her. "Unless you submit you will be abandoned like a heathen!" A threat terrible in that day. Joan answered resignedly: "I am a good Christian, properly baptized, and a good Christian I would die."

They tried to tempt her with an offer of a procession for the restoration of her health. To this she only whispered: "I greatly wish that the Church and the Catholics would pray for me."

They left her then. Whether she submitted or refused to submit, she was doomed. Their only real fear was that she would die and leave them.

Ah, why didn't she? But Joan was young, and of powerful physique. Spring had come back, the wonderful Norman spring. Her tower stood near the fields and such of their breath and glory as could creep into her narrow windows brought renewed strength to the fever-wasted prisoner. Perhaps she could even get a glimpse of meadows breaking into green. On the second of May she was able to be led before her judges for special admonition.

It was nothing new. Long charges were read to her and she

replied in her customary way. At one point she was warned that if she did not submit to the Church she would undergo punishment by fire. She said: "I will answer nothing further as to that; and if I saw fire before me I would say all that I say now and not otherwise." Next to this, on the margin of the page, Manchon wrote, "Proud response."

Asked if she would submit to the Pope, she answered: "Take me there and I will reply to him," and of that she would say nothing further. She had no vestige of faith in them and they knew it.

Again they warned her of the fires waiting her if she allowed herself to abandon the Church. She said: "You will never do what you say against me without evil befalling you, body and soul"—words calculated to send a shiver through that craven group and be long remembered.

If the reader is uncertain as to what Cauchon really wanted Joan to do, he is probably no worse off than was Cauchon himself. Whether she submitted or not he could convict her, and this he meant to do, his chief wish being to do it in a way that would give his public the least offense. After all, it might be better to condemn the Maid for *not* submitting to the Church. Everybody in that day belonged to the Church and held by it. For Joan to set herself against submission made her lawfully a public enemy. Of those who told the story later, the notaries as well as other witnesses believed that while Cauchon outwardly was urging Joan to submit she was by his orders being urged by Loiseleur to put no faith in the churchmen who, as he said, would not dare to do her any harm. All of which may well be true, though in any case Joan would hardly have answered other than she did.

The Torture Chamber

As we have seen, Joan from time to time had refused to reply to certain questions, especially those concerning her "secret" with the King. The bishop now decided to wring these from her under the threat of torture. Whether he really intended to torture her is uncertain. It is only certain that he would not have hesitated to do so had he thought such a course would make Joan confess. That it would damage him with the people of Rouen could, however, have held him back.

Whatever his intention, all was made ready. The torture chamber was in the main tower of the castle and here the instruments were laid out. Cauchon, with Loiseleur and other assistants, arrived and Massieu brought Joan dragging her chains —weakly enough, having risen from her bed of illness less than a fortnight before. Cauchon, addressing her, said:

"Joan, certain questions asked of you have been ignored by you or answered in a lying manner. On these questions we have information. If therefore you do not here and now avow the facts by answering these questions truly you will at once be put to torture with these instruments and by these men which you see before you."

Joan had probably never seen torture but its processes were well known to her. The word itself means to twist; among the instruments were those designed to distort, rack and shatter the entire human frame. If she hesitated, Cauchon's own record does not mention the fact. It reports her exact answer as follows: "Truly, if you should tear me limb from limb and part my soul from my body, I would not tell you anything more; and if I did tell you something, afterward I would say always that you made me say it by force!"

No torture chamber ever heard a more sublime answer.

She then spoke of the comfort she had received from the saints. She had asked her Voices if she would be burned and had been told that in this she must wait on our Lord, who would aid her.

The report further states that "seeing the callousness of her soul, the judges, fearing that the torments of torture would be of small profit to her, decided to wait for fuller advice." Three days later, thirteen of the assistants were appointed to vote on the matter. Ten of them, to their eternal credit, voted against torture. The remainder were for it. Two of these, Thomas de Courcelles and Aubert Morel, were religious zealots. The third was Nicolas Loiseleur, the spy, at that very moment posing as Joan's confessor and friend.

The last admonition

The University of Paris reported on the Twelve Articles, finding Joan guilty of blasphemy, divination, presumption, heresy and uttering false oaths. It recommended that she be abandoned to the civil judges to receive the sentence suited to her crime—that of death by fire. The Church could not pronounce that sentence; Joan must be judged and executed by the civil authorities. On the evidence as presented in the Twelve Articles—in view of the law and belief of that day and the fact that Joan was a deadly and dangerous enemy—the university's verdict could hardly have been other than it was.

Cauchon, however, was in no hurry to carry it out. He wanted to have the people with him as well as the university. His court, duly assembled, decided that Joan, once more and for the last time, should be admonished to submit to the Church. One of the assistants suggested that this should be done in public before the people, an idea which Cauchon promptly seized upon. The people must be shown an example of Joan's heresy and his own charitable pleading for repentance. If she still refused she would be burned at once; the executioner's cart would be waiting. If at the last moment she submitted, all the better. He knew Joan, and that such repentance would not last. She would *relapse!* Why, that was the best plan of all! She must be *driven to submit, then to relapse.* With everything in his hands he believed that he could bring this about and for the relapsed penitent who would dare to speak?

He would go softly, however. Joan must first be led before her judges and gently urged to return to the path of duty. She would of course refuse as heretofore, but by proceeding thus gradually the dignities would be preserved.

Joan did refuse. On May 23 she was led before a group of judges and one of them, Pierre Maurice, an earnest and probably sincere man, read her the substance of the Twelve Articles and the university's decision on each, addressing to her such persuasions and arguments as he could offer to one whom he must have known to be already doomed, whatever her reply. Joan listened patiently, as was her habit, until he had finished, then answered: "As to my deeds and my words, I refer to what I have said in the *procès* and will stand by it."

"Do you not think you are held to submit your words and deeds to the Church Militant, or to other than God?"

"What I have said and held during the *procès* I maintain still," replied Joan; then she added: "If I stood in judgment and saw the fire lit and the faggots burning and the executioner willing to put out the fire; and if I stood in the fire I would say nothing more and would hold to what I have said in the *procès*, until death."

And again Manchon wrote on the margin of his page, *Johannae responsio superba* (Joan's proud response). To this day it stands there, adding its touch of reality.

The *beau procès* had reached its official close. Cauchon pronounced the case concluded and assigned next day for the delivery of the sentence and for such further procedure "as should be required by law and right."

Joan, led back to her dungeon, had no reason to suppose that another day would not see her end. Her state of mind we can only dimly guess. Weakened by her illness she could still resist, as we have seen. She may still have expected aid from without— some miracle of rescue; she believed her Voices had promised that. She must have known that La Hire, eighteen miles below Rouen, had captured Louviers, which the English, while she lived, dared not attack. Remembering his former exploits she must at times have cherished the thought that this old comrade, in company with others—Dunois, Alençon, De Boussac, Poton, and the rest—had planned an assault, a swift wave of battle that would break over the walls of Rouen, dash her enemies aside and bear her away to freedom. Her heart bounded at any unusual noise in the street; she strained her ears for tumult of attack. But the ghastly hours went by without a sign or a word from those she had known.

Weakened and deserted, she began to waver. All the judges, even the more friendly, held her in sin, and now the great university. As she lay on her wretched bed she was not in a condition to think clearly on any course of action and later she said that her Voices told her she would yield. For a year she had been a captive and during five months had lain in this loathsome prison in chains. The physical and mental torture of her days and nights cannot be put into words or even imagined. That she was weakened, her mental balance disturbed, may be taken for granted. She was not a spirit but a human being, and the human being never lived of which this would not have been true. The marvel is that she escaped complete insanity.

At St.-Ouen

Next morning early—it was May 24, 1431—Bailiff Massieu arrived in Joan's prison to conduct her to the cemetery adjoining the church of St.-Ouen, where she was to be preached to; if she then still refused to recant and submit to the Church, she would be burned. Manchon was also present and one or two of the assistants, among them Loiseleur. Acting as her counsel, the spy now advised her to yield to the judges.

"Joan," he urged, "believe me, if you would be saved, take the dress of your sex and do all that you are commanded. Otherwise you are in peril of death. If you do what I tell you nothing bad will happen to you. You will have much that is good and you will be restored to the Church."

She was now taken to St.-Ouen, where two high platforms or scaffolds had been erected, on one of which was Cauchon and his assistants, the other being for Joan and the preacher, Erard. With Joan also were Massieu and Loiseleur; waiting near by with his cart was the executioner, ready to take her to the stake. A great crowd had assembled.

The Maid in chains labored up the steps of the platform and was directed to a stool. At once Erard began to preach to her. Bending over the despairing girl, he poured upon her head a torrent of accusation that dazed and bewildered her. There had never been in France, he said, such a monster as herself; she was a sorceress and a heretic; the King and clergy who had protected her, upholding the words and deeds of a woman defamed and full of dishonor, were no better than herself. Twice or oftener Erard repeated this charge, then fiercely raising his finger he shouted: "It is to thee, Joan, I am speaking and I say to thee that thy King is a heretic and a schismatic!"

Joan roused herself to defend the King who had betrayed and deserted her.

"By my faith, messire," she answered, "with all due reverence I dare say to you and to swear at the risk of my life that he is the most noble Christian of all Christians and best loves the faith and the Church. He is by no means what you say!"

Erard shouted to Massieu: "Make her keep still!"

For an hour the fierce, black-robed figure denounced the Maid and her King. On the adjoining platform sat other black-robed men with hard, unpitying faces. Below waited the executioner's cart and the soldiers. In all directions swarmed the multitudes, feeding upon the sight of the Maid, impressed by the preacher's storm of invective, eager for the promised spectacle. Overhead the sky was blue, the air was full of glorious spring when it was not easy to leave the world.

Bringing his seemingly endless sermon to a close, Erard began reading the charges which Joan was required to abjure and revoke if she would save herself from the flames. Exhausted in mind and body, she looked at him dazed, not understanding his words. Erard handed the paper to Massieu.

"Read and explain it to her," he said.

The paper contained six or seven lines, eight at most. Among other things, the Maid was required to promise that she would not wear arms nor man's dress nor have her hair cut short. As Massieu addressed Joan a tumult arose among the throng of spectators. Joan was being asked to sign something; they believed her about to escape. Many were glad; others were angry at the prospect of being cheated of their spectacle.

"Advise her to make abjuration—tell her to sign," said Erard to Massieu.

Massieu said something to Joan; Erard shouted at her that unless she signed forthwith she would be burned that very day. Joan confused, dimly comprehending, struggled to her feet, and, looking across to where sat Cauchon and the judges, said:

"Let all the things I have spoken and done be reported to Rome, to our holy father the Pope, to whom after God I refer them. As to my words and deeds I have said and done them through God. I lay them on nobody, neither on my King nor on any other. If there has been wrong in them I am to blame and no other."

The judges were on their feet, Cauchon shaking at her a menacing finger.

"Your case cannot be taken to the Pope!" he bellowed: "Rome is too far. We are your proper judges."

"I refer to God and our holy father the Pope," repeated the distracted Joan.

Cauchon had prepared two sentences. He produced the one of condemnation and began to read it. Loiseleur at Joan's ear was urging her to yield.

"Abjure, Joan; abjure and take woman's dress and be saved!" Erard was also urging her to sign, telling her she would thus be delivered from prison. Bewildered, distracted, overborne, understanding little and that vaguely, Joan at some point in the confusion about her said that if what they asked of her agreed with their consciences she would sign; saying further, according to Massieu who was nearest her, that she would rather sign than be burned.

Cauchon put aside the sentence he was reading and asked the English cardinal, Winchester, if Joan should be admitted to penitence. An English priest, believing the Maid was about to escape, called out to Cauchon that he was a traitor. "You lie!" Cauchon shouted back, adding that it was his duty to save body and soul. The commotion in the crowd was renewed; stones were thrown. The English priest was reprimanded by the cardinal. According to Aimond de Macy, who here appears for the last time, an English secretary now drew a paper from his sleeve and handed it to Joan.

"I can neither read nor write," she said.

A pen was put into her hand and she made a kind of circle, seeming to smile as she did so. The secretary took her hand and guided it to form a signature, or cross. Those who had seen the look on Joan's face called the abjuration a farce, as indeed it was, for her smile reflected a mind driven beyond the bounds of responsibility.

The paper that Joan signed was not the one that had been read to her by Massieu but another, more than seven times as long, containing much that she could not have heard. Except as it bears on the guilt of her enemies this is not very important. Joan that morning had reached a place where she would have signed whatever they put before her.

Cauchon now read the other sentence, which condemned

her to perpetual imprisonment, her fare to be the "bread of affliction and the water of sadness," in order, as he said, that she might weep for her transgressions and sin no more. Hard fate as this seemed it must have appeared welcome to Joan, who now believed that at least she would be taken from her dungeon and placed in the Church prisons with female attendance. A bitter disappointment awaited her. As they left the place of St.-Ouen, English soldiers insulted her and their leaders permitted it. The crawling Loiseleur whined: "Joan, you have done a good day's work. If God please, you have saved your soul."

"Well, then," she said anxiously, "you men of the Church, take me to your prisons and leave me no longer in the hands of these English."

But here Cauchon, speaking up, said: "Take her back where she came from."

Of all his acts this may rank as Cauchon's chief villainy.

That afternoon with certain of his assistants, the bishop visited Joan and explained to her the goodness of God and of the men of the Church in admitting her to pardon. Also that in case she sinned again she could have no further hope for forgiveness. They brought with them the woman's garments and Joan, retiring to such poor privacy as she had, put them on. The official record does not say that Joan begged them to place her in the Church prisons but that she did so is certain. Cauchon by no means intended to do that. In the Church prison the Maid might not relapse.

The Surrender

The story of what happened in Joan's prison during the next three days and nights will always be something of a mystery. It is only certain that to the unfortunate girl they were days and nights of horror. She told the friendly priests, Isambard and Ladvenu, that she had been attacked by her guards; also by another who had been admitted to her dungeon. Of this, Isambard said: "I saw her weeping, her face full of tears, and disfigured and outraged in such a manner that I was moved to pity and compassion." She was thus being driven to resume her male garments which had been kept handy in her cell. On the third morning one of the guards took away her woman's dress and another emptied a sack containing the man's clothing on her bed, saying: "Get up!" The woman's garments they put out of her reach.

The poor Maid pleaded that this was forbidden her, but to no purpose. She was finally obliged to put on the forbidden garments which meant her death. This was on Trinity Sunday, May 27, 1431.

The news that Joan had relapsed quickly reached Cauchon, who sent some of his assistants to make sure. But the English guards had lost faith in priests and drove them away. The bishop himself, with Isambard and others, came next morning and found her, truly enough, in male dress. She had taken it, she said, because it was more decent, being among men, and because they had not kept their promise that she should go to mass and be unchained. Asked if she had not abjured and sworn not to resume man's clothing, she replied that she would rather die than be in chains "but that if we would allow her to go to mass and would put her into a suitable prison where there was a woman, she would be good and do what the Church wished."

This is from the official record, the report of her enemies! The misery behind those calm official lines![1] She would rather die than be in chains. She had dragged their galling burden through all the fearful months. Even a small chafing weight can become almost unbearable. What, then, must this young girl loaded down with shackles have suffered. And her plea for

1. Recorder Manchon, who prepared the official report, later testified personally: "In my presence Joan was asked why she had resumed man's dress. She replied that she had done so to defend her decency because she had no safety in the dress of a woman, with her guards, etc."

a suitable prison—she was willing to promise anything for that! "I will be good," she told them; it is a child who speaks.

Had she heard her Voices since Thursday, the day at St.-Ouen, they asked? She replied that she had; that God through Saint Catherine and Saint Margaret had sent her word of the great pity of her sin in denying herself to save her life.

"Before Thursday my Voices had told me that I would do this. If I should say now that God did not send me I would again deny myself, for it is true that I was sent by God. It was through fear of the fire that I said what I did, having before my eyes the executioner ready with his cart."

Overwrought as she was it must have been in anguish and tears that she said these things.

"Do you believe your Voices to have been those of Saint Catherine and Saint Margaret?"

"I do, and that they came from God."

For the last time on the margin of his page the notary made a comment; only this time it is "*Responsio mortifera*" (fatal answer).

"What have you to say as to the sign of the crown?"

"Of all that I have told you the truth in the *procès*, the best that I knew. I did not intend to deny Saint Catherine and Saint Margaret and I would rather die at once than to endure any longer the torture of prison. If you will put me in a safe place where I am without fear, I will again put on woman's dress. For the rest I can do nothing."

They left her then, and to the Earl of Warwick and the crowd of English waiting outside, Cauchon said gayly: "Farewell, have good cheer! It is all over!"

Next day the bishop and forty of his assistants gathered in the chapel of the archbishop's palace to vote away her life. Cauchon read to them the report of his interview with Joan and asked for their verdict. Not one of those present, even of those who had been friendly to her and shrank now from what they were about to do, dared to offer a word in her favor. One after another, in that shadowy room, they voted for her death.

The Church itself could not take life. The form of their verdict was that Joan was to be handed over to the civil authorities with the request that they *deal with her tenderly*, such being the ghastly phrase which cloaked the sentence of death by fire. The bishop thanked them and spoke of the next step to be taken.

Martyrdom

Joan's days in prison were over. The night of the twenty-ninth of May, 1431, was the last she would spend there. She must have known this—that except for some miraculous rescue there could be no hope for her now. Did she still expect La Hire and the others to burst in at the last moment and bear her to safety, or some more directly divine intervention? Perhaps she did not even think of these things anymore, but, when her ruffian guards would allow it, gave her mind to prayer.

At moments she may have remembered phases of her brief life. She was only nineteen; a little more than two years before she had been spinning by her mother's side. In the midst of her anguish she could hardly fail to remember this and the Fairy Tree and the peaceful chapel of Bermont; the coming of the saints, and Vaucouleurs; the long night ride to Chinon; the King—Orléans and Patay. Had she ever ridden with her King to Reims at the head of a great cavalcade? Her faithful captains— where were they all? Oh, she was alone—her Voices . . .

It was early morning when Brother Martin Ladvenu came to tell her of the judges' verdict. She must die, he said—by fire.

At these words the tortured girl's strength gave way. How could they treat her so cruelly, she wailed, as to require this terrible death; and she said: "Oh, I appeal before God, the Great Judge, as to the wrongs and injuries done me!" and to Cauchon, who entered: "Bishop, I die through you."

Cauchon replied that she was to die because she had not held to her promise but returned to her first wickedness. She answered: "Alas, if you had placed me in the Church prisons that would not have happened. This is why I summon you before God!"

Pierre Maurice came, and she said to him: "Master Pierre, where shall I be tonight?"

And Maurice, who had meant to be kindly, replied: "Have you not good hope in the Lord, Joan?"

"Yes," she answered, "and God aiding, I will be in paradise."

She now asked for communion and with Cauchon's permission received it. It was first brought irreverently but Brother Ladvenu sent for lights and all that belonged to the service. Litanies were chanted, voices cried "Pray for her!" and there was a multitude of candles.

And now the executioner's cart came and, leaving the prison with Massieu and Brother Ladvenu, Joan entered it. She was clad in white, the "long garment" she had once asked for if brought to judgment. On her head was the square paper cap of the condemned. Surrounded by soldiers they set out for the Old Market, an open square already thronged with waiting people.

Joan of Arc began to pray—prayers, we are told, "so beautiful and devout" that those hearing them wept without ceasing. The wretched Loiseleur, struck with remorse, pushing from the crowd, tried to mount beside Joan to cry her pardon. Assailed by angry soldiers, but for Warwick he might have been killed.

By narrow streets the sorrowful procession reached the open market place, the soldiers pushing a way through the throng. Near a corner of the butchers' hall across from the church of St.-Sauveur, three temporary structures had been erected—two platforms, one each for the churchmen and civil judges, the third a high base of plaster surmounted by a grim post to which were attached chains, the stake. Around and about were heaped faggots; at its top was nailed a placard bearing such words as *Heretic, Relapsed, Blasphemer, Idolatress*—meaningless calumny.

Joan was now led to the platform on which sat the judges. The chosen preacher, Nicolas Midi, an assistant who had been especially active throughout the trial, began his sermon. It was a long and bitter tirade but the Maid heard it patiently to the end. She then began to pray so fervently and devoutly that all who listened were moved to tears. Of the priests she asked that each say a mass for her, and for herself and all others she asked God's pardon for her judges and the English, for the King of France and all the princes of the kingdom.

It was now about eleven o'clock and the soldiers, impatient at the delay, called out to Massieu: "How, priest, are you going to make us dine here?"

Joan finished her prayer and Cauchon read the Church sentence in which were repeated all the harsh, abusive terms they had applied to her so often. Closing with the request that she be dealt with gently, it abandoned her to the civil judge, whose faculties may have been beyond his control, for he did no more than wave her to the executioner with the words: "Do your duty."

And again was heard to say: "Go on—go on!"

Thus, with no other sentence than that pronounced by the Church, which was not a sentence of death but a mock recommendation to mercy, the Maid was seized by two soldiers and hurried to the stake.

From the high scaffold, Joan's gaze swept the thronging square and windows and roofs of the city of her captivity.

"Rouen! Rouen! Must I die here?" she cried; and another thought that she said: "Ah, Rouen, I fear you will suffer greatly for my death!"

And presently she begged for a cross. An English soldier broke a stick and tied it into a small cross which he handed up to her.

Taking it she kissed it tenderly, praying meanwhile, and placed it in her bosom between the flesh and the garment.

Then she asked to have a cross brought from a near-by church in order that she might always have it before her eyes until the last.

Brother Isambard hurried to the church and came back with the processional crucifix. Mounting the scaffold with it, for she was now chained to the stake, he held it to her lips.

But now the fire was lighted and as the flames crept up she begged him to descend, holding it always before her.

Many of the judges, unable to look upon their work, hurried from the place, some of them sobbing and uttering wild cries.

"I am not what their writings charge!" she wailed, meaning the cruel words on the placard over her and on the miter cap they had placed on her head.

And once she asked for holy water.

But then, as in the past, she called only on beings of light—Saint Michael and Saint Catherine and Saint Margaret.

And often she uttered the name of Jesus—more than six times the name of Jesus.

Some of those who heard it believed they saw that name written in the flames.

And one said that at the moment when she surrendered her spirit there appeared above her a white dove that flew toward France.

That no relic of her might be preserved the executioner scattered her ashes in the Seine. Later in the day he sought out Isambard and Ladvenu, overcome by remorse and fear.

"I shall never be saved," he said, "for I have burned a holy woman!"

A churchman said: "Would God my soul were where I believe the soul of that woman to be!"

XX

AFTERWARD

What came to Cauchon and others

Punishment did not fail to overtake those who had most fiercely hunted Joan to her doom. Immediately after the Maid's death, Cauchon and others held responsible for it were "pointed out with horror" by the people of Rouen, few of whom had been misled by the bishop's trickeries. Cauchon tried to counteract this by preparing a document in which certain of the assistants were made to say that Joan on the morning of her execution had acknowledged her Voices to be the work of evil spirits and the story of the sign a sinful invention. But as none of the assistants *signed* this document and none of the notaries would certify to their supposed testimony, it proved wasted effort on Cauchon's part. He never became Archbishop of Rouen. He was given the small Bishopric of Lisieux, where he added to his church a beautiful chapel of the Virgin, in expiation, it is said, of his sin against Joan. If he did this in hope of averting the Maid's prophecy that ill would befall him, his effort failed. He was struck with death while being shaved and though honorably laid in his tomb he was later excommunicated by the Church for defaulting in moneys due to Rome. His body was exhumed and thrown into an open ditch.

Cauchon's prosecutor, Jean d'Estivet, who not only spied on Joan but assailed her with evil names, was found dead in a slough at the gates of Rouen. The other spy, the miserable Loise- leur, fell into disrepute and, deprived of his office as canon of the church of Rouen, soon died. Nicolas Midi, who pursued the Maid even to the stake, where he denounced her almost in her last moments, became a leper and dragged out many fearful years before he found relief in death. What happened to the others of those who with Cauchon plotted Joan's destruction is not certain, but with these examples before them they must have lived in a state of dread.

Four years after Joan's martyrdom her chief enemy, Bedford, came to his end at the age of forty-six.

Georges de La Trémouille, King's counselor, the traitor who did more than any other man to bring about Joan's failure after Reims, deserves a fuller story.

Following the tragedy at Rouen there came a period of anarchy when the war became little more than a series of raids made by armed bands from both parties. Yet the cause for which Joan had died was never entirely lost sight of. Her captains were still fighting to rid French soil of English armies. Joan was dead but her spirit carried on. It would never again be true that two hundred English soldiers were equal to a thousand of the French. Orléans, Jargeau and Patay were not forgotten by either side. A leader who could unite the French armies as Joan had done was needed. The Constable, Arthur of Richemont, was the man; but though Joan had reconciled Charles to him little result could follow so long as La Trémouille was at Charles's ear. Richemont and La Trémouille, in fact, had been for years engaged in what was nothing less than a war of their own.

Finally in 1433 there came a dark night when Richemont concluded this matter in his own way. La Trémouille, then at Chinon, was lodged in the very tower of Coudray which Joan had occupied. Charles's nearest relatives had long wished to get rid of this evil adviser, especially Queen Yolande, who may have known how a door in the lower wall came to be left open, through which crept fifty of Richemont's men commanded by three knights, one of them a relative of La Trémouille himself.

La Trémouille, an excessively fat person, waking when a light flashed in his face, made a futile grab for a dagger at the head of his bed and was promptly stabbed by one of the leaders. The victim's great bulk saved his life. The glancing blade pierced only the gross tissue and did not find a vital part. A second thrust was prevented by his relative.

"He is my uncle," he said, "and as rich as he is fat. I will hold him for ransom."

La Trémouille was trussed like a chicken and carried to his nephew's castle, Montrésor. Charles, hearing next morning what had taken place, was only briefly disturbed. Calmed by his Queen, he appointed her brother, Charles of Anjou, to fill the office of La Trémouille. The latter paid his ransom but never returned to court.

The war now went forward with renewed vigor. Under Richemont and Dunois the armies were united. Even Charles, rid of his fat counselor, tried to be king. The Duke of Burgundy saw how affairs were going and became lukewarm in his love for the English. When Bedford died he delayed no longer but joined with Charles in a treaty which wrote the doom of England in France. Richemont and his army entered Paris and in November 1437, well within the seven years of Joan's prophecy, Charles VII made his formal entry. But for La Trémouille and his own paltry nature, Charles would have made that entry with Joan at his side immediately after Reims. Did he remember her in his hour of triumph? Perhaps; for Nicolas Midi, the same who had preached to Joan at the stake, forgiven and restored to favor and not yet a leper, now preached Charles's sermon of welcome to Paris!

One of the Maid's predictions still remained to be fulfilled—the enemy must go. By a lonely roadside far on the way to Cherbourg is a small stone column which marks the site of the Battle of Formigny, where on April 15, 1450, the English made their last stand in Normandy. Three years later they had lost everything but the single seaport of Calais, which they held by sufferance.

Joan had died but her spirit had carried on, her mission and her prophecy had been fulfilled.

Rehabilitation

When Joan had been dead more than twenty years, Charles VII decided to clear her name of the stain that had been put upon it when she had been sentenced to die as a heretic and a witch. It was not on the Maid's account that he wished to do this but on his own. The English had burned Joan to damage his title to the crown. A crown acquired through witchcraft was not legally held, they said; hence Charles was not the true King of France.

Charles and his advisers agreed that this would not do. To make it appear, however, that they acted for the sake of justice to the dead girl, claim for the revision of Joan's sentence was made in the name of her mother and two brothers, "anxious that her memory should be cleared of unmerited disgrace." Isabelle Romée was brought to Paris to plead in person at Notre Dame for her daughter's rehabilitation. Jacques d'Arc was no longer living, having died, it was said, from grief on hearing of his daughter's martyrdom.

The new trial opened in 1450 and continued at intervals

during six years. Sittings were held in Paris, Orléans, Domrémy and Rouen. Many were still alive who had known Joan and men and women in every walk of life were examined—all, with the possible exception of certain priests, eager to testify. Those who had played with her, little Hauviette and Mengette and many more—men and women now with children of their own; those who had marched with her—Dunois, Alençon, Louis de Contes, D'Aulon and many others; those who had helped to try her (though many were dead, Cauchon among them); those who had ministered to her last sorrowful needs—Massieu, Isambard and Ladvenu, told each his memories. All three of the notaries, Manchon and his two assistants, happily lived to tell their stories and from the various records, along with the records of Joan's own trial, it was clearly shown how little the Maid had deserved her fate.[1]

In the archbishop's palace at Rouen, where, twenty-five years earlier, Joan had been declared sorceress, idolatress, heretic and relapsed, on the seventh of July, 1456, in the presence of her brother Jean d'Arc du Lys, and the assembled court, a sentence was pronounced which bitterly censured her former judges, annulled their verdict and declared the Maid to be without sin, body and soul. Sermons and solemn processions were ordered at St.-Ouen, where she had been forced into an abjuration, and at the Old Market, where under the May sky she had found martyr-dom, the service at the Old Market including the planting of an expiatory cross.

Saint Joan

Of those of her family who survived Joan, something may be told. Her mother, Isabelle Romée, was pensioned

---

1. Today, after five hundred years, the reports of both trials are still carefully preserved. It is largely from them that our story of Joan has been written.

by the city of Orléans and died there in 1458, two years follow-
ing the verdict that restored her daughter to the full favor of the
Church. She was very religious and the patent of nobility which
Charles had conferred upon the family made her a lady of rank.
Altogether, she must have been held in high esteem and greatly
honored.

Joan's brothers, with their title, took the name of Du Lys
and lived as gentlemen. Jean du Lys in time succeeded De
Baudricourt as captain of Vaucouleurs, a distinction beyond his
wildest boyhood dreams. Pierre du Lys remained in Orléans. He
received a pension from that city and from its poet duke, Charles,
who after twenty-five years of captivity in England had returned
to his dominions. Both these brothers left descendants; some of
their blood may be found in France to this day.

Honest, lovable Durand Laxart, Joan's first convert and faithful support, lived many years. Whether he assumed the airs of
nobility under the King's grant, as was his right, we do not
know. He seems to have testified at the Rehabilitation as a
"laborer," so we may suppose he did not. He probably died as
he had lived, a loyal and upright peasant of Burey, leaving France
in his eternal debt.

When Joan had been dead well toward five hundred years
there was instituted a movement to declare her a saint. An ele-
ment in the Church opposed this, largely on the grounds that
she had not confided her visions and Voices to her priest or to
any churchman. Nevertheless, in 1904 she was designated "Ven-
erable"; in 1908–9 she was beatified and on May 16, 1920, at
the great church of St. Peter's in Rome, amid splendid cere-
monies, she was duly canonized, to take her place with those
whose Voices had directed her to the salvation of her people,
and to martyrdom.

Joan of Arc—Maid of France! Burned as a heretic and a witch,
long regarded as a half-legendary figure, today she lives again,
patron saint of her nation's armies, divine symbol of love and

sacrifice, not only in France but throughout Christendom. England, her old enemy, has set up statues of her. America has done the same and holds her in its heart.

> Across the night of history's blackest pages
> One name is scrolled as by a shaft of sun:
> Joan of Arc, the glory of the ages,
> Who battled hate, and lost—and, "losing, won."

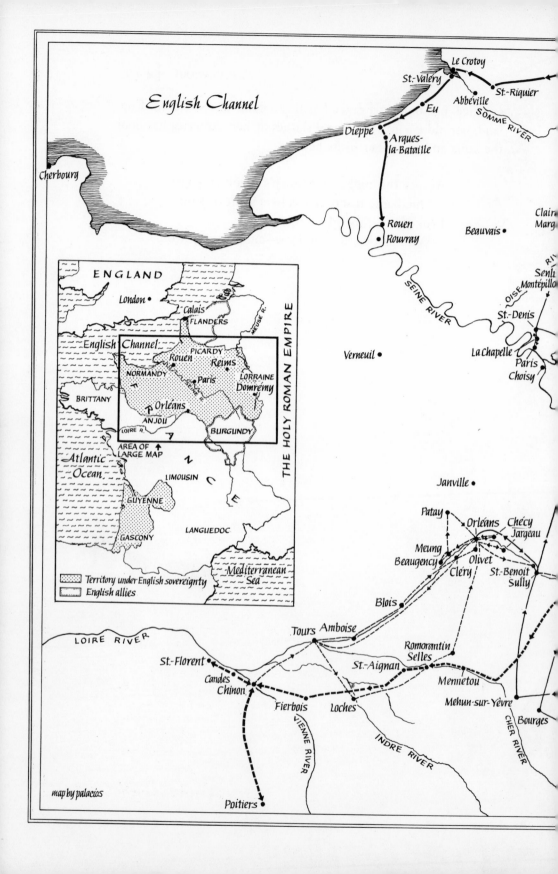

map by palacios

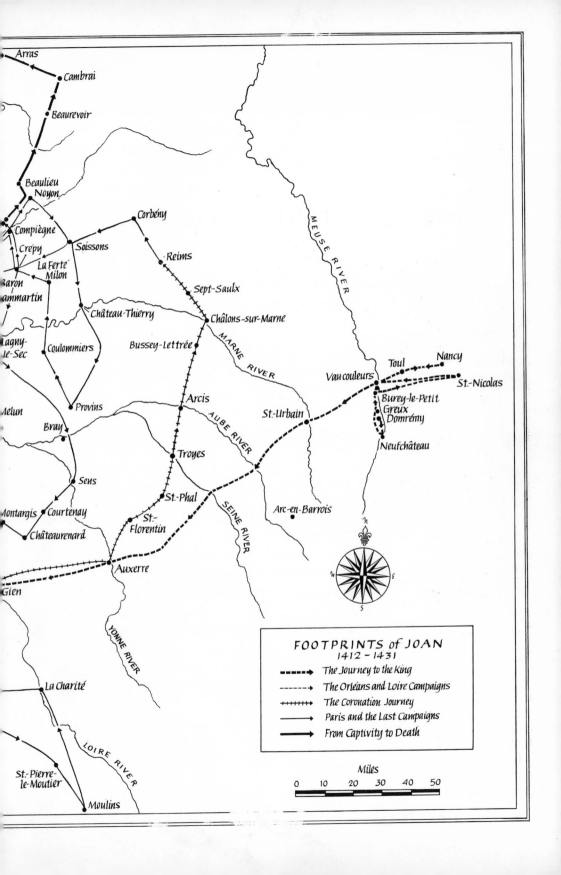

Arras

Cambrai

Beaurevoir

Beaulieu
Noyon

Compiègne
Crépy
Soissons
La Ferté
Milon
Baron
ammartin

Corbény

Reims

Sept-Saulx

Château-Thierry

Châlons-sur-Marne

Lagny-
le-Sec

Coulommiers

Bussey-Lettrée

MEUSE RIVER

Toul   Nancy
Vaucouleurs
St.-Nicolas

Provins

Arcis

St-Urbain

MARNE RIVER

Burey-le-Petit
Greux
Domrémy

Melun

Bray

Troyes

AUBE RIVER

Neufchâteau

Sens

St-Phal

Montargis   Courtenay

Châteaurenard

St.-
Florentin

SEINE RIVER

Arc-en-Barrois

Auxerre

Gien

YONNE RIVER

La Charité

LOIRE RIVER

St.-Pierre-
le-Moutier

Moulins

FOOTPRINTS of JOAN
1412 – 1431

- **------▶** The Journey to the King
- **------** The Orléans and Loire Campaigns
- **++++++** The Coronation Journey
- **——▶** Paris and the Last Campaigns
- **——▶** From Captivity to Death

Miles

0   10   20   30   40   50

XXI

FOOTPRINTS OF JOAN

The banks of the Meuse

To inquire one's way to Domrémy—to storybook land! How strange to be asking the road to a village in an enchanted valley, where once a little girl played under a Fairy Tree and on a summer's day in her father's garden saw a light and heard the voice of an angel. Even the way itself seems mysterious. You must wind among the hills, through still woods where no human form is seen, climbing, gradually climbing, until by and by you begin to descend to a wide valley with a river winding through—a hazy, purple valley, at one end a sleepy town, its church spires showing above the trees. This is Joan's land, the

NOTE: All references to towns, buildings, artifacts and features of the landscape throughout this chapter and the preceding chapters have been updated as far as possible, in the course of the text or in footnotes, to reflect changes since 1927, when the author set down his descriptions. [*ed.*]

[2 1 6]

valley of the Meuse; you are entering its southern gateway, Neufchâteau.

You remember that the Maid came to Neufchâteau. She was sixteen that summer and the Burgundians had raided Domrémy. The people, warned in time, fled with their flocks and goods to take refuge in this strong town, where they lodged with a good woman called La Rousse because of her glowing face and hair.

You would be glad to find the house of La Rousse but you will not be likely to do that; it was all too long ago. Of Joan in Neufchâteau, however, there remains something; two churches, in fact, both old when she saw them. Joan certainly prayed in these churches and they contain much that she could have seen. The lower chapel of St.-Nicolas was already three hundred years old when she came. Above, in one of the recesses, is a curious sculptured group, an "Entombment of Christ," which could have invited her wonder and adoration. St.-Christophe has the ancient nave and choir, little changed. Joan herself is represented there by a small replica of Pierson Martin's lovely statue of her, "Leaving the Distaff for the Sword," showing her about as she must have looked when she was there, her face full of light, her dress the blue bodice and red skirt she wore to Vaucouleurs. In the public square is a large statue of her, less intimate and beautiful.

But now we are on the road to Domrémy following the Meuse. On a hill to the left stands the great castle of Bourlemont and farther along comes Coussey, with its mossy church tower, familiar enough to the eyes of the children who looked down on it from the Fairy Tree.

Still following the shaded road and placid river we come at last to a stone bridge. Crossing it we reach a small, plain church and a curiously shaped house in rather pretentious grounds. Beyond them, and about it, is a humble village, as humble as it was when Joan knew it five hundred years ago. It has not changed its name—it is still Domrémy; the church is the one toward which she saw the light; it was in the adjoining garden that on a summer's day she heard the Voice.

Joan could hardly recognize the spot for there has been much change. The house which is called the "birthplace" is more pretentious than formerly, though in one room are some darkened beams said to be "original." Perhaps they are; one would be glad to believe they once supported the smoke-blackened ceiling above Joan's cradle. A cave-like cell is pointed out as "Joan's room."

Tradition says that Louis XI, son of Joan's King, restored the house, and outside above the doorway in old French is the inscription: "Long live King Louis" with some interesting shields, one bearing the device conferred on Joan and her family. The garden is not the kind of garden that Joan knew but whatever the house and grounds, there can be no doubt that it was here that she spent her childhood; here she received the first intimation of the work she was to do. The Brook of the Three Sources trickles by as it did then and, crossing the road, slips into the Meuse with a pleasant sound which her ear would find familiar.

In the little church are objects that Joan knew, must even have touched. One of them if genuine, and there is little reason to doubt it, is the ancient stone font in which she was baptized. Her fame began so early that the identity of such a relic could hardly have been lost. Today it is sacred—too sacred, it would seem, to remain in that perishing old church, though one would be sorry to see it taken elsewhere. In front of the church there is a statue of Joan; another, beautiful and impressive, stands in the grounds of the birthplace where also, in a small museum, is the primitive statue of Saint Margaret before which Joan is believed to have prayed.

In Domrémy itself Joan would find few landmarks but certain aspects of the life there would be familiar. It is more than five hundred years since she went about these streets or drove the flocks to pasture, just as others like her are driving them now. Some of the little shepherdesses spin with the distaff as they walk along, exactly as Joan did; most of them have fine features; many of them are named Jeanne or Jeannette and not a girl of Domrémy who does not carry a little glory in her breast and walk more proudly remembering Joan of Arc. In bystreets are the long-roofed stone houses of her time, in no way changed, only grown older and mossier as the centuries pass. In one of them little Mengette or Hauviette may have lived. The Bois Chenu still skirts the hillside above the road that leads to the site of the Fairy Tree but it is no longer deep and dark—not a proper shelter for wolves nor even for a reputed dragon. Below it, in June, strawberries still grow red and children gather them to eat with their small refreshments, which they would take to the Fairy Tree, only it is no longer there. It stood two hundred years after Joan left it but it is gone now and a rich, elaborate church stands in its place.

Looking out from the front of the church Joan would find the view not greatly changed. To the right rise the six distant towers of Bourlemont, as brave and fair as when the lord and his chatelaine used sometimes to assemble the children under the Fairy Tree. The old castle is still a home, though the family of Bourlemont vanished long ago. To the left, the villages of Domrémy, Greux and Maxey, mallowed by distance, must look about as they did then, while all between lies the hazy, purple valley of the Meuse—what it always was and will be, a place of dreams and unrealities. A little way down the hill is the spring where the children came to drink and where Joan sometimes heard the Voices. Clear and sparkling it flows from the hillside and sings and never grows old, and close by it the flowers bloom, such flowers as Joan and her playmates gathered to twine for the Fairy Tree or to lay before the pictures of the saints. Children today bring their lunches to the spring and drink the fresh, cold water which long ago was said to heal the sick and today is doubly blessed because of the little girl who once played there and spoke with angels.

A road from Greux and a byway and a path lead over the hill

to the chapel of Notre Dame de Bermont, Joan's favorite sanctuary. The chapel itself is much changed but it has an ancient bell and a primitive statue of the Virgin before which Joan is believed to have prayed. Joan would still love Bermont; it is so quiet there, so far from the affairs of men. The woods are still close about it and there are many birds, such as those that are believed to have eaten from her hand. At Bermont one feels very near to Joan.

Burey-le-Petit, which is now Burey-en-Vaux, has a house which is said to be that of Durand Laxart. One would be glad to believe that the home of this loyal soul had been preserved. No king ever did so much for France. Still following the Meuse we come at last to Vaucouleurs. It is not so far from Burey— three miles—and the level stretch between must have become very familiar to Joan during the winter weeks of her stay. One may imagine her trudging over the crusted road under heavy skies—disappointed but never dismayed, walking with presences which others could not see, holding fast by promises which others could not hear, words that meant the salvation of France.

At Vaucouleurs, Robert de Baudricourt's castle crowns the hill at the west and is reached by a steep climb. It is no longer a castle, but a ruin. Very little remains besides some walls, a few towers and arches and a replica of the chapel where Joan prayed. Yet with all the ruin, by some fortune the Port of France, through which the Maid and her little army rode into the winter night, remains almost intact, its arched gateway as perfect as at that great moment when they set their faces toward Chinon, where sat a disowned and discouraged King little dreaming that a peasant girl was on her way to bring him a crown.

The way to the King

One cannot even pretend to follow the route traveled by Joan and her knights to Gien. Keeping to the woods as they did, avoiding roads, bridges and towns because of the enemy, any surmise as to their course can be no more than the merest guess. What we know is that their first stop was at St.-Urbain, which is a few miles from Joinville, and that three days later Joan was in Auxerre. Of the Abbey of St.-Urbain not much remains. It is no longer an abbey and whatever is left of the building is used for storage. A beautiful gateway, probably the one by which Joan entered, still stands.

At Auxerre, however, most of what Joan knew remains unchanged. The great cathedral in which she heard mass crowns the hill above the river Yonne exactly as the Maid and De Metz saw it when they viewed it from their hidden camp and resolved to make their way to it for the consolation of divine service. The interior too must be about as it was then except for the kneeling statue of the Maid in memory and record of her visit. Joan, visiting Auxerre in the gathering dusk of a February evening, consciously saw little besides the church. The city today is of modern aspect but below the cathedral are old narrow streets about as they were when the Maid and her knight, risking capture, secretly followed them, to worship amid unsuspecting enemies.

Gien holds no positive landmark of Joan but the way beyond has many points of interest. Being no longer obliged to avoid the roads, the Maid's natural route was to reach the Cher and to follow it through Mennetou, Selles and St.-Aignan. At Mennetou by the roadside stands an ancient castle that may well have seen the little army pass, could even have given them shelter for the night. Also there are churches, some of them in crumbling ruin, where once Joan most certainly halted, however briefly. We know that she reached Ste.-Catherine-de-Fierbois and heard three masses at the famous shrine where a month later, by direction of her Voices, was found a buried sword. Above the altar there was a crudely carved image of Saint Catherine, to Joan very precious and holy. When a few years later the chapel was burned, this image was rescued. A beautiful Gothic church was soon built on the ancient site and the quaint figure of Saint Catherine again placed above the altar where it stands to this day, an object of much veneration. The house that served as Joan's lodging at Fierbois is little changed. It was built to resist time and is very handsome in its simple way. Still occupied, it is the home of the mayor of the village.

Ste.-Catherine-de-Fierbois, once famous, is today a neglected shrine; few travelers even know how to find it. Four miles north of St.-Maure, a little to the right of the road to Tours, it is easily reached by the motorist and is well worth a visit. The villagers themselves have not forgotten. Few and poor as they must be, in the little square before the church they have erected an imposing statue of the Maid and on its base are carved the names of those who died in the World Wars.

The old bridge over the Vienne which Joan crossed entering Chinon still stands. Like the great castle on the hill it was already centuries old, for it was built by Richard of the Lion Heart and had been crossed by knights and crusaders, and kings and queens, and fine ladies in tall hats and frills and farthingales, for more than two centuries.

Chinon was a strong city then, its stout walls packed with sharp-roofed houses, some of them very fine indeed. The progress of the centuries has swept away the walls and rebuilt many streets, yet something of what Joan saw still remains. The castle on the heights, though largely a ruin, is scarcely less imposing. Most of its battlements and at least some of its towers are as Joan saw them. The thin flat clock tower has withstood the centuries; even the house of the King has preserved something of its old outline. Altogether, the ruin must be nearly a quarter of a mile long and from the bridge presents one of the most striking pictures in France.

Its ruin is complete, none the less. Once through the entrance and you are under nothing but the sky with your feet on the grass. There is no longer a shelter, even for a fugitive king. It has become no more than a place for painting, for still seclusion, for dreaming in the sun.   •

There is enough to inspire dreams. For more than five hundred years it was a residence of kings. And all at once you are facing a wall in which halfway up there is a restored fireplace with a tablet which tells you that in this room Charles VII received Joan of Arc. It is no longer a room; it is just a wall, a fragment with vines matting its ruined edges. But at one corner, a little way from the fireplace, there are vestiges of a nook, an alcove, and it is easy to believe that it was here that Charles and Joan conversed apart when she gave him proof of her mission.

You cross a stone footbridge to Coudray, where Joan lodged, a large stone tower, its lower wall a full eleven feet through. Today it is roofless like the rest; cawing rooks circle above its emptiness. But the stairway she once ascended is unchanged and on the wall of her circular chamber is the outline of the fireplace whose cheer greeted her after her long winter journey. In this room once shone the "great light" that came with her Voices; here she fretted and prayed and sometimes wept, because of the dragging days.

Joan is still at Chinon a living presence, when the kings who for centuries reigned there are but dimly remembered. Henry Plantagenet, Richard Cœur de Lion, Louis IX, Richelieu—these great names are no more than whispered among the ruins, but all day and all the days is voiced the name of the peasant girl whose brief sojourn there meant the liberation of France.

From Chinon to Orléans

There are two roads by either of which Joan's cavalcade might have ridden from Chinon to Poitiers and on either route a castle where they could have passed the night spent on the journey. Our only certainty is that any existing castle in that neighborhood would today claim to be the true one, with a "Joan of Arc room," where the Maid slept.

There is more certainty at Poitiers. The house of Jean Rabateau (or Hôtel de la Rose as it was later called) where Joan lodged long since disappeared but its site was not forgotten. Today it is 53 Rue de la Cathédral, occupied by a small *magasin* (store) on the front of which is a tablet telling of Joan's stay. It has little to suggest the Maid but it is worth remembering that here Joan disputed with the doctors while curious or devout people filled the little street outside; here she promised to show her sign—declaring that her soldiers would fight and God would give the victory; here she dictated her first letter of warning that put fear into the English heart. A little way down the street we come to an open square and the great cathedral itself, one of the largest in France. Within, it is so lofty that the massive columns, many feet in thickness, seem slender as they mount upward. Joan attended the cathedral, a small figure in that vast place where today she has become one of the chief objects. On a high pedestal, her impressive statue faces that of Saint Peter across the aisle; upon it falls the tender light that once fell upon Joan herself.

Poitiers is an ancient city with other churches and buildings which Joan may have seen and not much that can certainly be identified. But at the Musée Augustin, 9 Rue Victor Hugo, there is a weather-beaten black stone preserved as sacred. It once stood on the corner opposite the home of Jean Rabateau, the stepping block from which Joan mounted her horse when she rode away.

It was at the Abbey of St.-Florent near Saumur that Joan visited Alençon's wife and mother. So little remains of the abbey today that one cannot be sure of its identity. At Saumur itself, however, an ancient castle, ancient even then, crowns the hill, impressive and beautiful. Joan must have seen it as she rode by; she may have visited it. On the road between Saumur and Chinon are other ancient castles while at Candes, halfway, there is the beautiful church of St.-Martin, built on the spot where the good saint who divided his cloak with a beggar ended his days. Joan on the way to St.-Florent would pass the entrance of this sanctuary. She would not pass, she would go in. One of the beautiful and holy objects of France, this church is little known; it can have changed very little since Joan was there.

At Tours, where the Maid went to prepare for battle, there are interesting reminders. At 16 Rue Briçonnet, the so-called, and *mis*-called, "House of Tristan," is believed by many to have been in 1429 the home of Jean du Puy and Eleanore de Paul, where Joan lodged. Then or earlier the house was in the Du Puy family but the record is not complete.

Joan went often to the beautiful cathedral of St.-Gatien and both herself and her banner received there special benedictions. The great church was already three hundred years old when she came and though not entirely completed much of it was then as it is today. Conspicuous in Tours are two great towers[1] seemingly a considerable distance apart, yet both were a part of the vast church of St.-Martin which in Joan's day was standing complete, an imposing structure.

Tours is a busy modern city; the street of the armorers is gone and cannot be certainly identified. Ancient streets there are in plenty and groups of buildings that carry memories of the days when the Maid with her knights and brothers and pages and faithful Jean d'Aulon went riding by or halted at the shop of the master workman who was building her "harness of war."

Riding to Blois by the north bank of the Loire the Maid passed through still-existing villages but they hold no memory of her. Opposite Amboise she could look across to a castle but not to the one we see there today; that noble structure, ancient as it appears, was not then built. It is the same at Blois; a part of the present magnificent château then existed but it has been completely changed. A ruined castle near by, the Maid could have seen, may even have occupied during her brief stay. The old abbey church of St.-Nicolas, much today as it was then, still remains the chief place of worship. That Joan assembled her

---

1. One, La Tour de Charlemagne, caved in in 1928. [*ed.*]

captains there[1] for penitence and prayer is highly probable. One
may imagine the lawless captains gathered about the ancient
altar and their astonishment as La Hire delivered his immortal
prayer.

Between Blois and Orléans the Maid's army made two camps,
the second of which must have been at Cléry, for not only is its
location right but it had and has a celebrated pilgrimage church,
a strong argument in its favor. From Cléry the army is believed
to have proceeded to Orléans by the way of Olivet, today a
dusty village without positive landmarks.

But now we are at Orléans, Joan's first great objective, with
no lack of reminders of her historic sojourn. The ancient city
walls are gone but at the corner of Rue des Africains and Rue
St.-Flore there stands a tower once a feature of the ramparts
and called *la Tour Blanche*. Diagonally across from it a tablet
over a factory entrance marks the site occupied by the home of
Joan's brother, Pierre d'Arc, by then known as Du Lys.

Joan attended the cathedral of Ste.-Croix, but the church
of that name today is very different from the one she knew,
which was wrecked by the Huguenots. Her own statue is the
most conspicuous feature of the place, rising as it does above
the main altar, while on all sides handsome modern stained-glass
windows tell her story. It is at Ste.-Croix on May 7 and 8 of
each year that splendid memorial services are held in her honor.
On the second day there starts from its entrance a grand procession of churchmen, soldiers and citizens to make the round
of the landmarks associated with her memory, returning at last
to the cathedral doors. It is the chief annual event of Orléans.

Near the post office, on the same street, is the house of
Jacques Boucher [now called la Maison de Jeanne d'Arc], where
Joan lodged. It is without doubt an old house and stands upon
the right spot near the site of the Regnart gate. It has been a
good deal restored, however, and the room pointed out as that
occupied by Joan is not very convincing. The house is rather

1. According to some sources, this took place at the church of St.-Sauveur,
which was destroyed in the nineteenth century. [*ed.*]

too spick and span for a fifteenth-century home. Yet Joan was certainly there and it was from one of these windows that Louis de Contes handed her her banner as she dashed away to her first battle.

Of the bastilles captured by the Maid there remain only some vestiges of the Tourelles, the strong towers that once stood at the south end of the bridge over the Loire. They were discovered not many years ago during some excavations and are to be found at the entrance to a tunnel, a little way above the present bridge, carefully outlined and identified. Just south of them, at the end of a short street, Rue Croix de la Pucelle, a small monument stands on or very near the spot where Joan was wounded. This is indeed worthwhile. Here rose the steep embankment; here through the long spring day she toiled with her soldiers to surmount it; here at last the gleaming white figure was struck down, only to return and plant her conquering banner against the wall. Busy people pass, apparently unnoticing. They have not forgotten, for the French remember, and this is hallowed ground.

Orléans has many statues of Joan. Of these the large equestrian figure by Foyatier on the Place Martroi, with its elaborate bas-reliefs, is the most conspicuous. Another is the well-known figure by the Princess Marie of Orléans in the court of the Hôtel de Ville. In the Musée des Beaux Arts are literally hundreds of statues, statuettes and pictures, works of imagination. Joan once spoke of seeing at Arras a picture of herself in armor but this has long since disappeared and in any case would have no value as a likeness. This museum, however, contains hundreds of relics of Joan's day; a piece of the ancient bridge, stone cannon balls, guns, coats of mail, axes, articles innumerable. The museum also has a head thought by many to have been modeled by a sculptor who had seen and studied Joan's features. It is called a head of a statue of Saint George but its features are unquestionably those of a young girl; its helmet such as she must have worn. Nothing about it suggests the ideal. It is a portrait of somebody; the more we look at it the more the conviction grows that its model was Joan of Arc. The face tells her story.

From Orléans to Patay

The Maid, leaving Orléans with the news of her victories, passed again by Cléry, this time with Dunois, and a tablet in the church records their visit there. During many hundreds of years kings and great churchmen of France made pilgrimages to the shrine of Our Lady of Cléry. The tablet bears many distinguished names, among them that of Saint Louis, who made a holy journey there before setting out for Jerusalem. Louis XI wore a leaden image of Our Lady of Cléry in his hat and when her church was partially destroyed by fire, restored it. Today his imposing tomb is one of the features of its handsome interior. In a near-by column rests the heart of Charles VIII. Few places in France are more worthy of a visit than this ancient and beautiful church.

Nothing identifies the spot near Tours where Joan greeted the King. It is in Loches that we next find her, in what was then a modern wing of a very ancient castle—a castle with a dark history in no way related to our story. That portion of the great structure associated with the Maid is called the château of Agnès Sorel [after a favorite of Charles VII], and it was in some portion of it that she pleaded with the King to come to Reims and receive his crown. This exquisite wing is today occupied by public offices and no one can point out with certainty the room assigned to the Maid. It is better to look at the outside of this portion of the château, realizing that as Joan saw it so it stands today. The castle of Loches must have become very familiar to Joan during those days when her wound was healing and she was urging Charles to action. It is a vast and somber place. She may have found it curious and interesting or she may have been too deeply absorbed in the work just ahead to give it much attention.

And now we come to Selles, and Joan is there and the King and Guy de Laval and many other persons of noble station, assembling for the great campaign that will end at Patay. And

Joan is ready to go and a big black horse is led out which refuses to let her come near him. "Lead him to the cross," she commands; and led to the cross that stands just before the near-by church, he becomes docile and permits her to mount; after which, her little ax in her hand, surrounded by her household, she rides away. The cross is no longer to be found but the old church is there and has changed little with the centuries. The open square about it must be much the same and some of the houses facing it are very old.

At Jargeau, the first conquest in this new campaign, there is no more than a bit of the ancient ramparts which the Maid conquered, but at Beaugency is the bridge she crossed; also the great square tower in which the English took refuge and near which she received the petition of Richemont and his lords. Beaugency is a very ancient town with houses, walls, gateways and churches old even before Joan's time. She probably gave them little attention—her hands were too full.

East of Beaugency are the low hills, scarcely more than rolling uplands, on one of which the French army formed the evening before Patay. Then comes Meung, to which she gave no more than a glance in passing, then Patay. Just where Patay was fought is not easy to decide. We look across the levels of wheat, wondering where it might be that La Hire led his terrific charge on Talbot, where the English formed at the hedge and were cut down, where Joan supported on her arm the head of the dying English soldier. The field was to the south of Patay; how far is not certain. Today the chief object on the plain is a windmill and as far as one can see are peaceful tides of wheat.

All these towns have fine statues of Joan in their public squares and their churches and their chief pride is that they were once details of a great battlefield where Joan of Arc checked English aggression in France.

It was immediately after Patay that Joan again met her King, this time at the abbey church of St.-Benoit between Châteauneuf and Sully, a famous shrine, one of France's oldest and most

curious landmarks. The centuries have done little to St.-Benoit.
The interior is much as Joan and Charles saw it and the impressive portico entrance, with its grotesque carvings, is only a little
more weatherworn than when the Maid said to the wavering
Charles: "Doubt not, you will gain all your kingdom and will
soon be crowned."

The way to Reims

The pilgrim who would follow today the way of
the coronation journey must for the greater part leave the high
road to one side and pursue narrow ways that wind among rolling lands less wooded and more richly cultivated than when
Joan and her King with their shining army passed by. Long war
had desolated it then—wars have desolated it since, but with
years of peace most of the scars have been overgrown.

Leaving Auxerre, of which this time Joan saw only the
outer walls, the army passed on to St.-Florentin, today a rather
sleepy town, but then with stout ramparts and a castle of which
little more than a fragment remains. The army camped at St.-
Florentin; also at St.-Phal, the old road to which goes twisting
among low hills with plenty of ancient villages that saw the
army pass. St.-Phal was just one of them but it had a near-by
stream which made it a desirable camping place. Probably St.-
Phal had never known such a day—has never known such a day
since—as that July afternoon when Joan's blaze of cavaliers rode
up the valley, followed by a seemingly endless train of soldiers
who forthwith began to pitch their camps and light their evening
fires. "Written at St.-Phal the fourth day of July." Thus closes
Joan's letter to the people of Troyes and the little town's claim
to immortality was assured. St.-Phal gave the lives of many of
its young men to the World Wars, and remembers them today
with a handsome shaft.

At Troyes Joan held a child at the font for baptism, though

whether in the cathedral of St.-Pierre, beautiful St.-Urbain or at the church of St.-Jean is not known. It was in St.-Jean that Henry of England had married Catherine of France in an effort to deprive Charles of his birthright. Today these churches have chapels and statues of Joan close to the main altar. Troyes has always been a rich and important city and though much changed has no lack of winding streets and ancient timbered houses, the occupants of which may once have seen Joan and her King ride by.

The road runs straight to Arcis, then again in a roundabout fashion until it comes at last to Bussey-Lettrée, another village, memorable because it was here that emissaries delivered to Charles the keys of Châlons. It was at Châlons that Joan found old friends who had come from Domrémy to pay respects to their little neighbor that now won battles and rode side by side with a king. There are some very old houses in Châlons; it may be that the very one in which Joan received her friends still stands but it is not known today. The Maid must have visited one or more of the ancient churches and in each is a worthy statue of her.

Following the winding road between the ancient villages, in most of which are timbered houses of that early day, it is not hard to imagine the humble and war-stricken people who gathered along the roadside to see the Maid and her army pass, many of them kneeling, for they truly believed her to be an angel of God. At Sept-Saulx, the next stop, the keys of Reims were delivered to Charles and from here on there must have been an increasing mass of the poor creatures eager only for a glimpse of the shining messenger who conducted the King to his sacrament and would give them rest from war.

How many times since then their land has been laid waste by battle! Twice in this century the rise of ground from which Joan caught her first glimpse of the cathedral presented an example of modern warfare, an exhibit of barbed wire and devastation. Distant hilltops, in her day green, were battered out of all semblance with bombardment. As to Reims itself, never in all the ages before was it the ruin of yesterday. World War I left it a mere heap of fragments, its splendid cathedral open to the winds, denuded of its rich reliefs, a poor, pathetic ghost of its former glory. Where Joan stood with her banner, where the King knelt to receive his crown, the war left a heap of rubbish and ruined entablature. Restoration has been completed but the cathedral of Reims that stood almost unchanged for seven hundred years, the cathedral that Joan saw, is gone forever.

In a corner of the great church are gathered some of its chief treasures, the most impressive among them being the Maid's statue by D'Epinay, the truest in spirit of all the hundreds that France can show. It is Joan as she might have stood there on that great day of fulfillment. Her dress is as it must have been; the face is of an indescribable beauty and of a sadness that wrings the heart. No wonder the assembly wept, if it was thus she appeared to them; for it is not Joan the conqueror, but Joan with the vision of all the days ahead, Joan the martyr and the saint.

From Reims to Compiègne

Corbény, Soissons, Château-Thierry, to which Joan and Charles rode after Reims, present few enough earlier memories. Corbény was left a mere waste of cinders and fragments and the lovely churches of Soissons were reduced almost to fragments by the First World War. Provins, however, where they arrived a few days later, is full of ancient things which consciously or unconsciously the Maid must have seen. At the church of St.-Quiriace on the hill, Joan and Charles attended mass; and a little way from the entrance is the so-called "Tower of Cæsar" which hardly could have escaped their notice. One cannot run amiss of old landmarks in Provins. There are even two hotels (one a hotel to this day), where she may have been a guest. Five hundred years ago Provins was a large, rich and strongly fortified city. Today, its population shrunken, its walls in ruins, it has become hardly more than a memory, a very beautiful memory, its vine-grown towers and crumbling gateways peacefully telling their story of battle and siege and how once on a summer day they gave welcome to Joan of Arc.

Wherever along the route there is an ancient church one may be certain that Joan was there, for prayer was her staff and weapon. She told her judges that she always confessed and took communion on entering a good town. At Coulommiers we may be sure of her at the church of St.-Denis, for she was three days in the town. La Ferté Milon also has an ancient church and above it on the hill is the ruin of a magnificent château, then quite new, constructed by the King's uncle Louis of Orléans fifteen years before his murder by John of Burgundy, but never finished. A large portion of the walls still stand, holding high in ornamental niches statues of the "nine *preuses*" or medieval heroines. The greatest heroine of them all lingered a brief time somewhere within what is now the great emptiness behind them, for the place is a mere shell open to the sky.

Between La Ferté Milon and the field of Montépilloy, Joan was at Crépy, Lagny-le-Sec, Dammartin and Baron, but only at the latter place is there any record of her visit. In the rare gothic church of this village is a kneeling statue of the Maid with a tablet which says that she took communion there before Montépilloy.

The village and ruined château of Montépilloy look out over the plain where the facing armies of Charles and Bedford skirmished the length of a summer day. Today the field is a billowing level of wheat. A fair ground it must have been for those brisk and bloody tournaments and what would one not give to see that fat knight in armor, Sir Georges de La Trémouille, tumble from his horse and be ignominiously dragged to safety! Five or six miles distant, at Senlis, in the beautiful garden of the abbey of St.-Vincent, is a handsome marble statue of the Maid, with an inscription which says:

"The fifteenth day of August, 1429, in the plain of Monté-pilloy in view of this belfry, ringing out for the Queen of Heaven, Saint Joan of Arc fought for France and for us."

It is at Paris that we next find Joan, making ready to assail the walls. La Chapelle, from which her attack was made, today within the city gates, has a church where she is said to have prayed before going to battle.

The scene of the assault at the gate of St.-Honoré was long ago built over and lost to memory. The spot where she fell cannot be identified but it is believed to be no great distance from the famous equestrian statue of her by Frémiet in the Place des Pyramides. For the Paris of that day covered a small area; its outer wall ran near where the Palais Royal now stands. Joan did not enter Paris but she is there today—in the churches, in the Pantheon, in many public places. Patron saint of the army, she is the city's idol.

The ancient church at St.-Denis has undergone many changes since Joan of Arc laid her armor on the altar of the Lady of Sorrows and rode away. The revolutionists of 1793 fell upon it with a kind of madness, desecrated its altars, emptied its royal tombs.

Joan's armor did not wait for revolutionists. Hardly was she on her way to the Loire before the town fell into the hands of the English and Burgundians, who captured and pillaged the church. They carried off the precious white armor but would hardly have destroyed it. In some English or French castle or museum or manor house it may exist to this day. It could be identified; there would be a patch on the shoulder, a break in the *cuissard*, the contour of the *cuirasse* would conform to the feminine outline. What a quest to seek for it!

St.-Denis has been restored and is worth a visit for its own sake and because Joan was there, but the royal tombs are empty and the altar upon which the Maid offered her white armor is not easy to choose.

Of the Maid's sorrowful trip back to the Loire with her

crowned King and her dwindling army, there is no trace today. One may imagine the disconsolate troops and captains fording the Yonne below Sens; filing by castles, today crumbling to ruin, that mark the route by Courtenay, Châteaurenard and Montargis, the Maid and Charles halting now and again at mossy churches; but the tale of these things is lost.

After which comes St.-Pierre-le-Moutier, her next scene of action, and here still stands a considerable fragment—a tower —of the ramparts she captured with the aid of her "fifty thousand," a victory commemorated by a statue in the public square. St.-Pierre is memorable and worthy of a visit. Also La Charité, where she failed and where today a stretch of the old rampart surrounds a flourishing vineyard, effectively keeping out trespassers, just as long ago it defied Joan and her ill-provisioned army. Like Paris, La Charité honors Joan in its churches, though she failed to surmount its walls.

During her final stay below the Loire, Joan when not in action was for the most part with Charles's court, which was sometimes set up at Bourges, sometimes at Mehun-sur-Yèvre and again at La Trémouille's great château at Sully. At Mehun-sur-Yèvre, where Charles conferred rank on Joan and her family, there stands a beautiful fragment of the royal château. Below it are green meadows and a winding stream, the whole completing a picture of tender and romantic beauty, the kind of thing one finds everywhere in France. A little distance away is an ancient city gateway through which the Maid and her King more than once rode side by side.

La Trémouille's great château at Sully on the Loire still stands. It is one of the few castles that have been continuously occupied and though the centuries have made changes a number of its earlier towers are reflected in the river and moat precisely as they where when Joan was there. Somewhere in one of them she doubtless lodged during the tedious day of her unwilling residence.

At Bourges there remains the great cathedral with magnificent thirteenth-century windows unchanged since Joan saw them. The Maid must have visited the cathedral and today she stands there in marble, her hands clasped in prayer. She wears a helmet and a long military cape; the face is one of great spirituality. It is Joan as she might have looked when she rode away from Sully, knowing as she must have known that the end was closing in.

At Lagny and Melun we find the Maid again in action but the landmarks are not many. In the square in front of the church at Lagny is a statue which holds aloft the sword taken from Franquet d'Arras on the plains of Vaire. It was doubtless at the church opposite that the supposed miracle of the resurrected child occurred. Joan herself spoke of it as being at Notre Dame but Lagny seems to have had no church by that name. Of Joan's stay at Melun we know little more than that she received here warning of her approaching capture. This happened on the moats, long since disappeared. In Melun there is in fact an ancient church called Notre Dame, which she probably confused with the one at Lagny. That she visited the church at Melun is certain; it may well have been her Gethsemane.

Compiègne, the little city on the Oise for which Joan gave her liberty, has always been the center of a battleground. During World War I bomb and shell tore away many an ancient landmark but most escaped injury. The church of St.-Jacques, where Joan heard mass before her sortie, was damaged by shell fire. It has, however, been restored; her fine memorial altar there was uninjured. In the main square, facing the Hôtel de Ville, the Maid has an impressive bronze statue. Fully armed, she waves her banner aloft and on the base are her words: "I will go to my good friends of Compiègne." During the World Wars bombs fell a little distance away but the Maid's statue was not struck.

The street along which Joan rode for the last time is named for her. The gateway through which she passed to her final charge is gone; also the bridge across which, a flashing figure at the head of her five hundred, she swept to strike the camp at Margny. Margny has no vestiges of a camp or of the ancient *boulevards* but on a house facing the quay is a tablet which tells that it was near this spot Joan was captured. The court at the back contains vestiges of the terminal arches of the ancient bridge which the *boulevard* joined; the Maid was forced from that embankment into the lower meadows. The ground has been filled to the bend of the arches so that the level of her capture is a good ten feet below the surface. Only the visible portions of the old stone work are left to bear witness to the spot where, in the crush and clamor of battle, Joan of Arc was borne down by the enemies of France.

Where the footprints end

The trail of Joan's last sad journeyings is none too plainly marked. The brick castle of John of Luxemburg at Beaulieu, though struck more than once during the World Wars, survives in part and is still a habitation. Whether Joan ever occupied any room in the remaining portion is not certainly known. One of the present humble tenants may point out a dark underground place as her prison but it is highly improbable that it was there. Except that he sold her, the Maid was well enough treated by Luxemburg. A little way from the castle there stood until World War I a bronze statue of the Maid of which only the base is left. It bears this inscription: "First stop on the way to Rouen."

Her next stop, Beaurevoir, was also in the war district. The village itself was almost completely destroyed but a little way to the west of it on a low hill stands a shell-shattered remnant called the Tower of Joan of Arc. The castle of John of Luxemburg doubtless stood on the slight eminence, and tradition says that from this tower the captive girl made her desperate leap for freedom.

In the village itself there was formerly a statue of the Maid, but here, as at Beaulieu, the enemy carried it off for the bronze. Only the scarred base remains. Nothing is to be found today at Cambrai or at war-smitten Arras, though we have it from her own lips that she passed that way.

It is different at "Drugy Farm"; the small tower that became a one-night prison for the Maid of France is little changed. It is all that is left of Drugy castle and at present forms the corner support of a large Picardy farmhouse. The small tower may have been higher but the part which survives undoubtedly sheltered the weary Joan after a long day of riding in chains. A tablet over the door records the fact of her sojourn. Soldiers lodged in it during World War I.

Between Drugy and Le Crotoy, a little way beyond Noyelles, near Morlay, the road passes a small but exquisite church, today the ruin of a hundred years. Joan saw it in its glory; they may have let her pray there.

Of the great square fortress on the bleak Picardy headland of Le Crotoy, where Joan was kept for a month or more, one can find no more than a bit of the foundation. An old chronicle says of her departure:

> She bade adieu to those of the castle of Crotoy, who mourned her departure, for she had greatly consoled them. One sees yet the room where she slept, which since that time commands the respect of those who visit it.

But this was written long ago. There remains today no trace of Joan's tower. Le Crotoy has become a modern summer resort. Portions of the ancient church are of Joan's time but except the harbor and the great sea beyond there remains nothing else that she could have seen.

Along the road from Le Crotoy to Rouen by way of Eu and Dieppe, only the castle of Arques-la-Bataille, a little way below Dieppe, has been identified with her journey. Here, in an imposing ruin, the so-called castle of Henry IV, the guide will try to point out the location of Joan's room. Imagination can make little of the crumbling heap and the eye wanders to the distant slopes on which the captive's gaze once rested.

Between Arques and Rouen are Norman villages with small ancient churches, some of which certainly saw the Maid and her guards pass by. And from the hills above Rouen one may still look down on the spires of the cathedral and of St.-Ouen, on the sweep of river and huddled houses, though of the vast assembly of towers which formed the Château of Philip Augustus, the Maid's last prison and the scene of her trial, only one remains.

Aside from the exteriors of the cathedral and St.-Ouen, there cannot be much in modern Rouen that Joan consciously saw. Both these churches have undergone change. The vast abbey once connected with St.-Ouen has disappeared. The cemetery near the entrance, scene of the abjuration, has been replaced by a garden.

A portion of the archbishop's palace is of Joan's time, and on one façade of it, facing the street, are two tablets side by side. One of them, with the date, Tuesday, the twenty-ninth of May, 1431, tells how she was cited there to the scaffold; the other, with the date, Wednesday, the seventh of July, 1456, tells how on the same spot was delivered the verdict that cleared her name of undeserved blemish.

The "tower near the fields" where Joan endured five months of unspeakable misery vanished long ago. The one existing remnant of the great castle of Philip Augustus is the great donjon (or main tower), much restored, where the Maid withstood the threat of torture. This is now a museum and has many visitors. Somewhere within its walls Joan defied the thumbscrew and the

rack. On a near-by street is a tablet which marks the supposed
site of the tower that was her prison. A commercial building
stands there today and it does not seem to be in the right location
to have been "near the fields."

The street plan of Rouen has changed somewhat with the
centuries, so that it is no longer easy to trace the way of sorrow
which led from the Maid's prison to the Old Market where she
died. Streets have been straightened and others obliterated to
form the wide thoroughfare which today bears her name.
Leaving this, one finds the changes have been fewer, and here
and there are tottering Norman houses from whose narrow
windows, one sorrowful morning, looked pitying women as
the savior of France passed by.

Following the Street of the Good Children, so called then
and now, we come to the Street of the Prison, which leads
directly to the Old Market, still a market where busy people
throng in and out on necessary errands. The church of St.-
Sauveur is gone but about on the old site stands a butchers'
hall and at its corner a tablet set in the pavement bears the words:

JEANNE D'ARC

30 MAI

1431

Another tablet, on the building itself, shows the ancient plan
of the place and tells more fully the story. This is France's holy
ground. The cross that was once planted here long since disappeared and Rouen, in shame and sorrow trying to forget, did
not replace it. Later, in another square, the city set up a memorial
fountain which in turn was replaced by a pretentious statue.
The simple tablet in the pavement is better. Somehow it expresses
the straightforward girl of Domrémy who here under a May
sky gave her life for France.

JOAN OF ARC:

A CHRONOLOGY

January 6, 1412	Joan is born to Isabelle Romée and Jacques d'Arc in Domrémy, Lorraine, France.
September, 1424	Joan hears her Voices for the first time.
December, 1428	Joan goes to Robert de Baudricourt at Vaucouleurs to ask his help in seeking out the court of the Dauphin.
March 6, 1429	Joan has her first interview with the Dauphin in his castle at Chinon on the Loire.
late March	Joan is examined for heresy at Poitiers and found to be "of good faith."
April 20	Joan leaves Chinon for Orléans.
April 24	At Tours Joan's "white armor" and banner are made.
April 29	Joan and her soldiers enter Orléans.
May 8	The English are driven from Orléans.
June 12	Joan and her army capture Jargeau.
June 16	Joan drives the English from Beaugency.
June 18	Joan defeats the English at Patay.
June 29	Joan and her army set out from Gien with the Dauphin, to conduct him to Reims.
early July	The city of Troyes opens its gates to the coronation army.
July 17	The Dauphin is crowned King Charles VII at Reims, with Joan in close attendance.
August 14	Near the plains of Montépilloy, Joan's army skirmishes with that of the Duke of Bedford, commander of the English in Paris.

August 26	Joan and her army arrive at St.-Denis, near the gates of Paris.
September 7	Charles VII joins the army at St.-Denis.
September 8	Joan attacks Paris and is wounded.
September 11	Joan offers her "white armor" on the altar of Saint Denis, patron saint of France.
September 21	Joan, the King and the army return to Gien on the Loire.
early November	Joan captures St.-Pierre-le-Moutier.
December	Charles VII confers nobility on Joan and her family.
(late March, 1430)	The "flight from Sully": Joan leaves the Loire on her last campaign.
April 17	Melun surrenders to Joan.
May 23	While fighting the English near Compiègne, Joan is captured.
June–November	Joan is imprisoned in the castle of Beaulieu by John, Duke of Luxemburg, who finally sells her to the English.
late December	Joan arrives in Rouen, a prisoner in chains.
February 21, 1431	Bishop Cauchon summons Joan for the first time before his tribunal of sixty judges.
end of March	Cauchon attempts to make Joan confess to a list of Seventy Articles supposedly based on her testimony.
May 2	Joan is threatened with torture.
May 24	Joan is driven into signing a confession.
May 30, 1431	Joan is condemned and excommunicated as a heretic and is turned over to the English rulers of Rouen, who burn her at the stake.
July 7, 1456	A new trial censures Joan's former judges and affirms her innocence.
May 16, 1920	Joan is canonized at St. Peter's Cathedral in Rome.

INDEX

Names of cities and towns are italicized.